Reviews of Melissa Benn (2012) *Sch*

'This is a tremendous book ...
about the most important policy ᴜᵢᵥ.
book's publication marks her out as one of Britain's toreₘᵤ.
advocates of comprehensive education.'
Anthony Seldon, *The Observer*

'If you read just one book on education this year, then
make sure it's *School Wars* by Melissa Benn. Brilliantly
researched and compellingly written.'
**Roy Blatchford, Director of the
National Education Trust**

'An important watershed. It is a clear-sighted re-statement
of why universal, comprehensive education is – obviously –
the best option. It should ... be taken as a rallying call to
the left.'
Phil Beadle, *The Independent*

'An exceptionally well-informed, cogent, and spirited account
of the debates over secondary education in Britain.'
Stefan Collini, *The Nation*

'Well written and passionate.'
Frances Beckett, *The New Statesman*

'What Melissa Benn's superb, evidence based history of
the educational battleground during the second half of
the last century proves, is that today comprehensives are
mainly Good or Outstanding (according to schools inspector
OFSTED), are getting higher standards in national tests
and exam results, and are delivering social mobility ...

Benn's statistics prove that comprehensives are best –
and can become even better ... While identifying a
deep-seated Tory and New Labour love affair with the
independent sector, she forensically shows how Labour

politicians have obstructed the case for a radical overhaul of our secondary school system.'

Neil Fletcher, *Camden New Journal*

'*School Wars* is a book that touches nerves in the English education system. It probes the way in which differences for young people show themselves and exposes so much of the rhetoric in a world where we take extreme variation in opportunity and outcome for granted. Melissa Benn raises the sorts of questions that have needed answering for a long time and offers much food for thought to those with responsibility at every level.'

Mick Waters, former director of Curriculum at the British Qualifications and Curriculum Authority

'As Melissa Benn's superb book makes clear, however, a focus on the reactionary, back-to-basics language of such reforms threatens to obscure a vastly more important and unprecedented change to the way our nation's schools work: the importation of the language and culture of private industry, with its relentless focus on quantity (that is to say, formal results), rather than the quality of a rounded education . . .

Over the course of its brief but tightly argued two hundred pages, Benn makes clear that the real threat is not the fusty conservatives calling for a return to rote learning, but the breakneck speed at which the business world is being enmeshed with the provision of our children's education. As she makes clear, these changes are bound to issues of class and social stratification that are far more subtle, and worrying, than they appear at first glance . . .

School Wars provides ample evidence that an approach to education inspired by the free market, and founded on a competition in which the dice are loaded, is deleterious, regressive and unjust. If this book is read as widely as it deserves to be, the author will have started a conversation that might just arrest this trajectory.'

Andrew Fleming, *Ceasefire* magazine

'Melissa Benn, in her enthralling though depressing account of current and recent educational policy, is quite clear that the legacy of both the Coalition and, indeed, the previous Labour government is the gradual abandonment of the key principles of comprehensive education to which all parties once appeared to subscribe. Indeed, this process is accelerating, not simply through the introduction of "free" schools or academies, but by the way grammar schools are allowed to open new satellites in a crude circumvention of the existing prohibition on new schools. There is nothing subtle about the current assault on comprehensives.

Benn's book is a powerful combination of history, contemporary analysis and prospectus, seeking to explain why comprehensives have fallen out of favour in recent years and why England needs a revival of the comprehensive ideal. Much of the book deals with the contrast between the aspirations of the past and the realities of the present. Her main contention, however, is that the comprehensive principle was never properly applied and as a result comprehensive schools never gained the necessary cache and popular support they needed to succeed ...

Melissa Benn passionately believes that the new direction in English education is not only dangerous but frightening leading, potentially, not to better-educated citizens prospering in a cohesive and equitable society but an "increasingly fragmented, mistrustful and divided nation, controlled rather than enlightened, dependent on the unstable whim of private or religious enterprise" (p. 204). This is both a timely analysis and a serious warning which no-one should ignore.'

Deian Hopkin, National Library of Wales

'Melissa Benn has produced an impressive study of the rapidly changing school system in contemporary Britain . . . this book should be a wake-up call for so many of the population who may not realise just how much the school system has been fragmented . . . Benn asks people to consider "whether our public services are to be run by a democratic state, or whether they are to be put out to tender". She has done a service in drawing our attention to the motives of many behind these recent changes.'

Clive Griggs, *Forum* magazine,
University of Brighton

'. . . a beautifully written and concise history of comprehensive education. She has pieced together a complex story that begins with the early stirrings of discontent against the eleven plus and selection, unfolds as a popular crusade for equal opportunity and democratic education, and eventually becomes a chronicle of lost illusions and ideological warfare . . . *School Wars* aims to encourage those who hope for an inclusive, openhearted and effective system . . . But this is war . . . '

Bernard Barker, Institute of Education,
***Forum* magazine**

'Melissa Benn has written a timely, useful and highly readable account of issues around education in Britain from the end of the Second World War up to the present day. She concludes with some thoughts about what can be done to develop a better, more equitable approach for the future

. . . Coalition's abolition of local admission forums is a retrograde step. The ability of local authorities to plan pupil admission in their area has been grotesquely undermined by the expansion of the academy programme and the launch of free schools. "Take away the democratic elements of school planning and you are left with widespread anarchy . . . you get a series of mini-fiefdoms controlled by powerful interests . . ."'

David Lister, *The Chartist*

'Melissa Benn's book conveys a sense of urgency, which is just as well since it comes "at a pivotal and highly dangerous point" in the history of English education. "The choice and diversity" revolution begun by Thatcher and pursued by Blair is now being advanced "with manic zeal" by Cameron's Tory-led coalition . . . the Book is clearly heart-felt, much of it based on her own experience of the state education system . . . It is evangelistic – in the best sense of that word. I thoroughly commend *School Wars* to all those who, like me, are concerned about the imminent destruction of our state education system.'

Derek Gillard, *Forum* magazine

'Melissa Benn has given the defenders of equitable education for the whole community, not just the chosen few, some powerful ammunition.'

Nicholas Murray, *Unite* magazine

The Truth About Our Schools

Opinions about comprehensive education are often made into easy-to-swallow sound bites by media and politicians alike, and whilst the benefits of a genuinely comprehensive education for all pupils are obvious, untruths have unwittingly evolved into hard facts. Based on Melissa Benn and Janet Downs' work as part of the pioneering Local Schools Network, *The Truth About Our Schools* calls for us to urgently and articulately challenge unquestioned myths about state education. Benn and Downs have meticulously built an argument for its still enormously vital role, and rigorously challenge assumptions that:

- Comprehensive education has failed
- Local authorities control and hold back schools
- Choice, competition and markets are the route to educational success
- Choice will improve education in England: the free school model
- Academies raise standards
- Teachers don't need qualifications
- Private schools have the magic DNA
- Progressive education lowers standards

Anyone who thinks that comprehensive education cannot deliver, that local authorities are the chief block to improving our school system, that competition and markets are the route to educational success and that private schools hold the magic DNA that can simply be transferred to other state schools, will have their beliefs shaken by this blisteringly incisive book.

Melissa Benn is a journalist and author, a campaigner for high-quality comprehensive education and a founder of the Local Schools Network.

Janet Downs is a retired secondary school teacher. She is now an education researcher and blogs regularly on the Local Schools Network.

The Truth About Our Schools

Exposing the myths, exploring the evidence

Melissa Benn and Janet Downs

Routledge
Taylor & Francis Group

LONDON AND NEW YORK

First published 2016
by Routledge
2 Park Square, Milton Park, Abingdon, Oxon OX14 4RN

and by Routledge
711 Third Avenue, New York, NY 10017

Routledge is an imprint of the Taylor & Francis Group, an informa business

British Library Cataloguing in Publication Data
A catalogue record for this book is available from the British
Library

Library of Congress Cataloging in Publication Data
Names: Benn, Melissa.
Title: The truth about our schools : exposing the myths, exploring the
    evidence / Melissa Benn and Janet Downs.
Description: New York, NY : Routledge, 2016.
Identifiers: LCCN 2015023395 I ISBN 9781138937161 (hardback) I
    ISBN 9781138937178 (pbk.) I ISBN 9781315658674 (e-book)
Subjects: LCSH: Education—Great Britain.
Classification: LCC LA632 .B436 2016 I DDC 370.941—dc23
LC record available at http://lccn.loc.gov/2015023395

ISBN: 978-1-138-93716-1 (hbk)
ISBN: 978-1-138-93717-8 (pbk)
ISBN: 978-1-315-65867-4 (ebk)

Typeset in Celeste
by Swales & Willis Ltd, Exeter, Devon, UK

Printed and bound in Great Britain by
TJ International Ltd, Padstow, Cornwall

Contents

Contents

Foreword

Over the course of my educational career – beginning as a classroom teacher in 1964 and including my work as an administrator in local authorities, a researcher in universities and even, for a brief spell, a Her Majesty's Inspector of schools – I have been appalled at the frequency with which obviously untrue comments about comprehensive education have been disseminated by commentators and repeatedly parroted by politicians and the media. For those, like me, who have taught in a secondary modern as well as in a comprehensive school, the benefits of a system designed for *all* pupils are obvious.

Rashly, during the second half of the twentieth century teachers in comprehensive schools tended to assume that the benefits of higher expectations and the increased provision of opportunities for achievement made available to the nation's children must be self-evident. Sadly, it seems we underestimated the power of those who – committed to private or to selective education for an elite group – were, and remain, determined to sabotage the comprehensive principle.

Fifty years on, we have seemingly made little progress. The idea that all children are equally worthy of high quality

education in common schools is still resisted and comprehensive education denigrated. Those untrue comments
have hardened into myths. Furthermore, the situation
has been exacerbated by the creation, by ministers from
all political parties, of academies and free schools which
enjoy enhanced funding and greater freedoms.

It is enormously helpful, therefore, that the *Local Schools
Network* has taken on the task of challenging these perva-
sive myths. This publication is the fruit of their labours.
Seven of the most common myths have been investigated
and the evidence for them meticulously evaluated.

The results are clear. Comprehensive schooling has
proved itself to be more successful than a market in
which pupils, teachers and an array of different types of
schools are forced into never-ending competition. What
the evidence reveals is that a national system of comprehensive schools – overseen by democratically elected
local authorities and staffed by qualified teachers, free to
innovate and to develop better (even progressive) ways of
teaching and learning, is what our society needs. This, in
many ways, is a similar message to that revealed by the
OECD's Programme for International Assessment (PISA).

The irony is that our society had the basis of near-national
system of comprehensive schooling which worked. But,
since the Education Act of 1988, so many ministers,
largely on the basis of the myths described here, have
done their best to wreck it. We now need citizens to lobby
their political representatives to ensure that future education policy is made on the basis of evidence such as that
provided by this excellent publication.

Professor Peter Mortimore
Former Director of the Institute of Education,
University of London and Professor of Education,
University of Southern Denmark

Comprehensive education has failed

Reading today's newspapers or listening to or watching our media, you could be forgiven for believing that comprehensive education has been a widespread and resounding failure in this country. Contemporary commentary, from the boldest headlines to the passing casual phrase, has a repetitive one-note quality: 'Schoolchildren "being failed by comprehensive education"';[1] 'Comprehensive schools failing poor pupils';[2] 'Comprehensive schools have failed the working class';[3] 'What about the comprehensive failures?';[4] 'A choice in which the only option ends up being the failing local comprehensive is no choice at all'.[5] According to one recent critique, it is 'generally regarded' as a 'disaster'.[6]

Even articles that purport to be sympathetic to non-selective education will nonetheless employ emotive language – 'Kent *boasts* the highest number of grammar schools'[7] – or metaphors more appropriate to the battlefield as when referring to 'grammar schools which *survived* the *drive* towards comprehensive education'.[8] One well-known memoir of a comprehensive education bears the rather worrying title, *Comp: A Survivor's Tale*.[9] Even some Labour leaders have been tempted to use unhelpfully

1

emotive imagery – former Prime Minister Tony Blair talked about the phasing out of selective education as an act 'pretty close to academic vandalism'.[10] Other arguments verge on the patently ridiculous, such as columnist Peter Hitchen's claim that 'the comprehensive system is anti-education'[11] or novelist Tony Parson's bizarre assertion, taking the battlefield metaphor to its bloodiest extreme, that going to a comprehensive is 'a start in life right up there with dying at the Somme'.[12]

But such assumptions and distortions simply don't stand up to careful scrutiny. Worse, they obscure a sober assessment of everything from the history of our school system to the structural nature of the labour market, the relationship between economic and educational inequality and the reality of thousands of state schools today. (It is perhaps no coincidence that the majority of editors and prominent commentators who promote an anti-comprehensive rhetoric are privately educated or have chosen private or selective education for their own children.)

Meanwhile, almost every *social* problem, from the impact of poverty and rising inequality on educational outcomes to classrooms in poor repair is laid at the door of state education, particularly non-selective schools, and despite compelling expert evidence to the contrary, most commentators still recklessly assert that comprehensive reform is responsible for the stalling of 'social mobility' in the UK. But as Diane Ravitch writes in response to similar political assaults on public (state-funded) education in the United States, 'public education is . . . not "broken". Public education is in a crisis only so far as society is and only as far as this . . . narrative of crisis has destabilized it.'[13]

That is why, in place of the half-truths that pass for objective reporting, we need to draw on the wealth of evidence and human examples that tell a very different story. From this we will see that far from having bred educational failure, the (still unfinished) comprehensive revolution has laid the basis for the potential educational success of the vast majority of young people today.

The principle of comprehensive education is simple. Every child, whatever their social background or apparent intelligence or talents, should have equal access to a well-resourced, broad and balanced education from the earliest years to the age of 18 (from 2015, the legal age for participation in education or training). It is morally and practically wrong to decide a child's potential, ability or direction in life before puberty. All young people should be well taught and wisely guided throughout adolescence so that they can (begin to) pursue their true passions and talents. Comprehensive education also sends out an important message about children being educated *together*: that regardless of class, faith, ethnic background, prior attainment, all children should walk through the same gates to school.

This interlinked set of simple but powerful ideas forms the basis of some of the most successful education systems in the world including Canada, Finland, Hong Kong, Singapore, New Zealand, Japan and South Korea. International studies confirm that comprehensive systems and all-ability schools are the most likely to narrow the educational attainment between social classes and that the more and the earlier that an education system divides its children by so-called 'academic ability', the greater the gap between the resultant achievements of children from different social backgrounds. The OECD found that 'Early student selection has a negative impact on students assigned to lower tracks and exacerbates inequities, without raising average performance. Early student selection should be deferred to upper secondary education while reinforcing comprehensive schooling.'[14]

Where the selective principle still operates within the UK – 15 local authorities still retain the 11+ and 164 grammars remain – the evidence strongly suggests that it largely benefits the affluent, widens the gulf between the better and less well-off and does long-term harm to the economic prospects of the poorer members of those communities in which selective systems exist.[15] Grammars increase social divides and harm the educational and economic chances of the majority of the population in the area where they are located: 'Individuals who do not make it to the grammar school do worse than they would have done if they had grown up in an area with a comprehensive school system.'[16]

Comprehensive reform was the result of growing dissatisfaction with the 1944 settlement which, while establishing the crucial right to universal free education, was structured around the separation of children at puberty according to their presumed talents and ability. The 11+ exam decided if a child was to be sent to an academically-oriented grammar school or a secondary modern where the curriculum was less demanding and few, if any, exams and qualifications were on offer. A third option – the technical schools – never really took off in this post-war period, although the idea is enjoying a kind of revival with the new studio schools and University Technical Colleges.

The 11+ divided young people before puberty but with lifetime consequences and largely along class lines. The long-term effect of failing the 11+ has been described by John Prescott: 'The message was that suddenly you are less than they are. It tends to leave you with an inferiority complex.'[17] Recent research by a website offering learning for those aged 50+ found that this effect is common even 40 years on:

> Of those who failed the 11+, 36 per cent said they still 'lacked the confidence' to undertake further education and training courses, while 13 per cent insisted the experience 'put them off learning for life'. Some 45 per cent

of adults with poor 11+ results said they still carried 'negative feelings with them into their fifties, sixties and beyond', it was revealed.[18]

We need to look much more closely, then, at the so-called 'golden age' of the grammar schools in the 1950s. Although a minority of lower middle class and an even smaller proportion of working-class children did gain entry to grammar schools, 'places tended to go to the sons and daughters of professional business men/women'.[19] Not only were the majority of working-class children channeled into the less well-resourced and less well-regarded secondary moderns, but as former head Adrian Elliott recounts in his book on state education since the 1950s, academic results in the grammar schools themselves were under par. Those working-class children who did get into a grammar often gained fewer qualifications and left school much earlier.[20] As Elliott states,

> According to the Crowther Report in the late '50s a staggering 38 per cent of grammar school pupils failed to achieve more than three passes at O-level . . . It is clear that of the entire cohort of 16-year-olds at this time, only about 9 per cent achieved five or more O-levels and that less than half of those who attended grammar schools reached this benchmark.[21]

These figures, say Elliott, were national averages and so included some of the most high-achieving grammars of the period.

Opposition to the 11+ grew during the 1950s as academics increasingly questioned the evidential basis of the exam itself and ever larger numbers of vocal middle-class parents became unhappy when their children were consigned to clearly 'inferior schools'. The journalist Simon Jenkins has written about the 'gilded myth' of the grammars, and reminds us that

Comprehensive education has failed

> At political meetings at the end of the 1960s, the—then education spokesman—Edward Boyle was torn limb from limb by conservative voters, infuriated that their children who had 'failed' the 11+ were being sent to secondary moderns, along with 70–80 per cent of each age group. They had regarded the grammars as 'their schools'. The 11+, they said, lost them the 1964 election and would lose them every one until it was abolished. Margaret Thatcher recognised this as has every Tory party in practice ever since.[22]

Simon Jenkins also reminds us of the bi-partisan nature of reform during the late 1960s and 1970s with both Conservative and Labour local authorities backing the move to 'all-in' schools. Across the political spectrum it was realised that, properly organised, and sufficiently resourced, 'all-in' schools could give many more children the chance to thrive, academically and socially.

Comprehensive reform was never fully achieved. Even today, in 2014, a significant number of grammars remain, together with a small but powerful private sector that educates 7 per cent of the population. Nevertheless, from the '60s onwards, comprehensive reform had a major impact on the chances of the majority. First, most children in this country were not told that they were failures before they had reached puberty and therefore were deliberately to be consigned to second-rate schools. Second, the advent of comprehensive education endowed those same young people, who would previously have been written off as wholly without skills or talents, with the chance to acquire a range of knowledge and qualifications and the confidence to continue enjoying learning. Coupled with a progressively higher school leaving age, it gave many more young people the chance to gain qualifications so that the percentage of young people gaining five O-levels (or GCSEs) rose from 23 per cent in 1976 to 81 per cent in 2008.[23]

According to Brian Simon, an early advocate of comprehensive education,

> the concept of a common curriculum for all . . . was a major objective of the whole comprehensive reform movement of the 1960s and 1970s [and earlier]. This movement was primarily concerned to prevent shutting off access to full life opportunities for considerable proportions of the nation's youth.[24]

This it did, in spectacular fashion. The number of students in education at age 17 grew from 31 per cent in 1977 to 76 per cent in 2011 and those achieving a degree rose from 68,000 in 1981 to 331,000 in 2010, an almost fivefold increase.[25] Both the percentage and absolute number of working-class men and women who went to university in the 1970s increased for the first time since the 1930s.[26]

Jenny Chapman, the Labour MP for Darlington, spoke of the human side of this expansion, in a debate on social mobility in the House of Commons in 2010:

> five or six years ago there were one or two wards where a young woman of eighteen or nineteen would be more likely to be a mother than to be a student in higher education. I can report with great pride that this is no longer the case. Teenage pregnancies are reducing, and participation in higher education in those wards [is] improving. That needs to be taken into account when we discuss social mobility.

We hear too little of these stories. Even today, when relatively few grammars remain, and those that do overwhelmingly educate the affluent, we are constantly told (wrongly) that it is only selective education that changes working-class lives. However, relatively recent research undertaken by Chris Cook, at the *Financial Times*, in 2012, confirms the evidence that selective education actually harms the vast majority of poorer children. Cook found that in selective areas, the most disadvantaged students were less likely to get the top scores and far more likely to get low scores than in areas of comprehensive education. Cook also found that, for the very richest in society, there was a definite benefit to attending grammar schools. Those in the top 5 per cent by income did better than those in non-selective areas. However those in the bottom 50 per cent for income did, overall, worse in selective areas.[27]

Unsurprisingly then, the stress associated with the 11+ seems greater than ever and success is arguably as much about the advantages conferred by family background, including parents' ability to pay for tutoring, as any 'innate ability'. There are reports of children attending 11+ coaching at 5am in the morning and parents paying as much as £5,000 in tuition to get their children through the 11+. More than six out of ten children receive some form of tutoring.[28] Of those parents using the web site www.elevenplusexams.co.uk, 63 per cent agreed that private tutoring 'significantly enhanced' their child's chances in the 11+.

Recent attempts to 'tutor-proof' the test in order to boost the chances of poor and ethnic minority students have come under critical scrutiny from campaign groups. The Buckinghamshire based 'Local, Equal, Excellent' has uncovered data, obtained through Freedom of Information requests, which casts doubt on the claims of those who say the test boosts the chance of less advantaged students. According to a report of the campaign group's findings in the TES:

> The data suggests that children of black Caribbean and mixed white/black Caribbean heritage in the town of High Wycombe did particularly badly in the first year the exams [were] sat, in September 2013. The combined

success rate for these groups fell from 15 per cent to
5 per cent. Children of Pakistani heritage also appeared
to do worse in the town: they made up 13 per cent of
children gaining grammar school places in the year
prior to the new test, but just 11 per cent under the
first year of the new test.[29]

In selective authorities, passing the 11+ can become the
'be-all and end-all' to anxious parents. Journalist Lucy
Cavendish described her experience of coaching her son:
'To be frank, it turned me into an obsessed loon. In fact,
I became almost deranged.' Continuing, she describes the
effect on parents going into appeals:

> These women have already been through the wringer.
> They've probably coached their children to within an
> inch of their lives. They have worried themselves silly as
> their poor children went into that quiet room last October
> and took the tests. They've endured weeks of waiting for
> the results. This is their last chance. Their children failed
> the test – probably just by a few points. All they can do
> now is use every single plea they can muster to gain a
> much-coveted place at one of our local grammar schools.
> [They feel as if it] is their last chance saloon.[30]

As we have argued, out-of-date perceptions of comprehensive education, fostered by an often hostile press, has
projected an overall image of a mediocre, failing sector.
There has been little discussion of the fact that the continu-
ation of overtly or covertly selective education, in large
parts of the country, has in some areas, at some periods
of the recent past, rendered many local 'comprehensives'
anything but – particularly those in areas of high deprivation,
which have struggled to succeed in the face of multiple
challenges, particularly in periods of economic hardship.
And while some local authorities provide excellent support

to local schools, others have not been so successful. All local authorities faced a particularly difficult time during the 1980s under a central government that neither believed in high quality comprehensive education nor was willing to invest in it. Since 1997 however governments, both Labour and Conservative led, have been more committed to improving non-selective education and parental confidence has increased accordingly. Combined with a number of creative locally based schemes for collaboration and improvement such as the London and National Challenge, many non-selective schools in deprived areas have become among the most successful state schools in the country.[31]

For all this, we still hear too little of the achievements of state education in general and non-selective education in particular year. For example, nearly half of the intake of MPs following the 2015 election were educated at comprehensive schools. In particular, there is no established public narrative concerning the role of comprehensive education over the last few decades in significantly improving the life chances of thousands of working-class women and men. As Selina Todd, author, history lecturer and Vice Principal of St Hilda's College, Oxford, argues, 'It wasn't grammar schools that assisted working-class people to get to university, but the introduction of comprehensive schools.'[32] Todd, herself from a working-class background and educated at a comprehensive, has written elsewhere that comprehensives show students that

> academic success is founded on hard work and effort, not on family background and wealth—the criteria for entry to private schools—or the innate 'talent' that selective schools claim to identify. Most importantly, comprehensives still provide far more students with the opportunity to do A-levels and apply to university than do private or state selective schools.

Despite the lack of a unified comprehensive system, public support for the idea of local 'all-in' schools, and the performance of the vast majority of these schools, remained resilient from the 1960s to 2010, particularly after a sustained period of investment. Ofsted's 2011 Annual Report noted that 94 per cent of parents completing their questionnaire agreed that they were happy with their children's education, up from 93 per cent the previous year.[33]

Politicians over time have recognised the de facto popularity with parents of a good local school, open to all, even if many cannot bring themselves to endorse the non-selective principle or use the 'c' word. The Education Act of 2002 declared that one of the key characteristics of the new academies should be that they provide 'education for pupils of different abilities who are wholly and mainly drawn from the area in which the school is situated'.[34]

On coming to power in 2010, it was clear that the Tory-led coalition recognised the potential popular appeal of comprehensive education. Former Education Secretary Michael Gove frequently declared his belief in the idea of 'non-selective excellence' and the current head of Ofsted, Sir Michael Wilshaw, former head of a highly successful comprehensive in East London, has frequently declared his implacable opposition to grammar schools 'stuffed full of middle class kids'.[35] The coalition's flagship policy of free schools and academies draws directly on the comprehensive legacy with its commitment to a 'good local school for all', founded on all-ability entry, and improving the education of the children from the poorest backgrounds.

As Sam Freedman, former adviser to Michael Gove wrote, on the day of Gove's (dramatic) departure from the Department for Education in July 2014,

> perhaps his greatest achievement has been to normalise comprehensive education for the Conservative party; to shift the argument from 'saving' a few bright poor

kids through grammar schools or assisted places to creating a genuinely world class system for all. In time I suspect that will be more widely recognised than it is now.[36]

However, during the period of Coalition government from 2010–2015, pressure was building up in support of expansion of the grammar school estate, both from small groups of parents within selective areas and Tory back-benchers who have made it clear that they want to see a return to academic selection. It remains to be seen how responsive the Conservative government, elected in May 2015, will be to these varied pressures and how much it will hold to the Cameron/Gove vision of a high quality school for all.

Let us briefly puncture a related myth: the charge persistently levelled at modern comprehensive education that it is a key driver in the demise of 'social mobility' and prime cause of growing economic inequality.

Several reports and commissions, set up since the turn of the twenty-first century, have focused on this issue, creating 'a political consensus . . . in which stalling social mobility is seen as a distinct problem [from which it] then follows, in every political account, that the solution to the problem is education'.[37] Such a 'consensus' is then endlessly used to argue for the return of grammar schools and the separation of children into vocational and aca-demic streams (if not at 11, then at 14).

But what if such a consensus is just plain wrong? The first of the series of papers to put the argument on the link between social mobility and education was the Aldridge Report, a discussion document published by the Policy and Evaluation Unit in 2001 under Tony Blair's premiership.[38] This suggested that social mobility, as defined in terms of earnings, had fallen between the late 1950s and 1970, and that Britain had become a less class-fluid society. For many Labour politicians this confirmed the importance of New Labour's commitment to 'education, education, education' while Conservatives latched onto the Aldridge findings to argue the slow-down was caused by the closure of grammar schools.

A more publicly influential LSE-Sutton Trust report, published in 2005, also argued that children born to poor families were less likely to break free of their background and fulfil their potential than they were in the past.[39] Comparing two boys from different backgrounds – both born in 1958, both of whom left school in the 1970s – it found the boy from the richer family born in 1958 earned in adulthood on average 17.5 per cent more; by the 1970s, the difference had leapt to 25 per cent. The report also confirmed that the relationship between family income and children's higher education attainment had grown stronger between cohorts completing their education in the 1970s and that 'the expansion in higher education in Britain has benefited those from richer backgrounds far more than poorer young people'.

However, few seemed to notice that the Sutton Trust report focused on the *birth* dates of the two respective cohorts – 1958 and 1970 – and that both sets of boys (and it was only boys) came to puberty and the start of their all-important secondary career, at a time when comprehensive education was well entrenched. Also, no-one seemed to notice that rates of social mobility were much higher in other countries, like Canada and the Nordic states, where comprehensive education was well established, suggesting that the problem may lie elsewhere. For some commentators, such as Tim Luckhurst writing in *The Times,* the Sutton Trust report confirmed 'only a blend of ideological zeal and intellectual dishonesty could now defend the comprehensive system'.[40]

Experts now argue that there is a fundamental misunderstanding at the heart of the concept of social mobility

13

and the role that education plays in it. In his seminal 2012 paper, 'Understanding—and misunderstanding—social mobility in Britain', Professor John Goldthorpe argues that increased social mobility in the post-war period was more a case of more room being found at the top of the economy, than a tale of a (now defunct) education system powering individuals to its summit.[41] The structure of the labour market changed markedly during the twentieth century with a rapid growth of professional employment after the Second World War which then slowed down. Professional and managerial jobs stopped expanding and, at the same time, women with greater educational qualifications began to enter the labour market.

According to Goldthorpe, 'no decline in mobility, either absolute or relative, occurred in the late 20th century'. Moreover, the rate of *relative* social mobility, which measures the chances of a given person escaping their class origins, has not changed for a century. After reviewing all the evidence, Philip Collins of *The Times* observed that 'This argument often finds its way into public debate in a fractious and unenlightening exchange about grammar schools. It is true that absolute social mobility started to decline about the time that comprehensive schools replaced grammar schools . . .' But the really interesting thing, he goes on to say, is that neither a selective nor comprehensive system had any real impact on rates of social mobility.[42]

Bernard Barker and Kate Hoskins came to a similar conclusion in their recent, more qualitative, study of 88 students in two high-achieving state schools. Despite excellent teaching, good results and high expectations for all pupils (from both the school, and the children themselves) class inequalities and destinations appeared to remain largely unchanged. Barker and Hoskins attribute this to a complex set of factors including the way that school organisation, from primary school onwards, reproduces class position, to individual students' wish for personal happiness as much as material success, commitment to their families, including areas of work associated with particular family histories. Official explanations, from across the political spectrum, of education's role in promoting social mobility fall far short of the complex reality of human lives.[43] Furthermore, as Selina Todd argued in the 2014 Caroline Benn Memorial Lecture, excessive concentration on the questionable goal of social mobility takes social *inequality* for granted and risks re-enforcing it.[44]

In short, to regard education as the *main* way in which disadvantaged pupils can rise economically is profoundly flawed. These changes will not happen unless other social and economic policies are in place. One reason for this, as Goldthorpe argues, is that 'when education standards generally improve, the more advantaged parents will still use their wealth to maintain their children's competitive edge'. At the same time, lack of educational success is less of a handicap for advantaged children because they can access support networks unavailable to disadvantaged children who don't succeed. These strategies prevent 'downward mobility', the logical consequence of a genuinely fluid and open society, but an aspect of the process that no politician dare even contemplate, let alone publicly advocate. Of course, if downward mobility were to be considered allowable – even as a subject for serious discussion – then selective and private education would surely be identified as one of the key props used to shore up the privileges of the children of the already affluent, whatever their so-called 'natural ability'.

Far from comprehensive education hindering the chances of poorer children, our long-established and deeply hierarchical education system appears, even now, to exacerbate inequality. In 2010, Barnardo's, the children's charity, found that sophisticated admissions policies within the state sector led to marked social and economic segregation and prevented the entry of poorer children into higher attaining schools.[45] An OECD adult skills survey recently found the gap between disadvantaged and advantaged children in the UK to be very wide – wider than in most other OECD countries, and clearly associated with inequality in income distribution. 'In England/Northern Ireland (UK) . . . social background has a major impact on literacy skills.'[46]

According to Mary Bousted, general secretary of the Association of Teachers and Lecturers (ATL),

> Schools simply cannot compensate for the serious and lasting effects of child poverty . . . If politicians are to do more than preach about social mobility or wring their hands about the educational attainment of poor children, they need to address the root cause of educational inequality: poverty . . . School teachers and support staff work every day to alleviate the burden that poverty places on the life chances of poor children. They do not need lectures on social mobility from politicians whose policies increase child poverty and blight poor children's futures.[47]

Professor Goldthorpe agrees. He argues that 'equality of opportunity' is unlikely to be effective unless 'class-linked inequalities of condition' are significantly reduced. Social mobility is more marked in Scandinavian countries where policies are directed at reducing income differences through taxation and welfare policies combined with 'strong trade unionism and employment protection'. According to OECD head, Andreas Schleicher – once described by former Education Secretary, Michael Gove, as the 'most important man' in UK education – results from the triennial PISA tests found education systems are more likely to succeed if education policy is aligned with other public policies – if they they are coherent, sustained and consistently implemented.[48]

A wide range of voices across the political spectrum now agree that not only is comprehensive education consistent with excellence but as a school system it forms the best basis for more equal and cohesive social relations. Writing to *The Guardian* in 2010, Selina Todd, vice principal of St Hilda's Oxford, spoke of how her college welcomes

> applications from comprehensive school students, not because these candidates can do well in spite of their school, but because their education offers them an excellent foundation for university. Many comprehensives offer imaginative lessons, encourage independent study, and provide an unparalleled social education. Being educated alongside pupils from a wide range of backgrounds gives these candidates the ability to negotiate cultural and social difference in debate, and the confidence to relate abstract or scholarly theory to the wider society in which they live.

Todd's argument is supported by *Daily Mail* journalist Sarah Vine, wife of the former Education Secretary, Michael Gove – the first ever Conservative education secretary to choose a state school for his child. Writing about her own comprehensive education Vine said that unlike private schools,

> they provided me with a broad education . . . in life. And in the realisation that you shouldn't judge people by their clothes, or where they live, but by who they really are regardless of circumstances; that kids studying to be hairdressers deserve as much respect as those wanting to be rocket scientists.[49]

Comprehensive education has failed

For all the myth-making about comprehensive education, few public figures would seriously suggest – or at least, not publicly – the return of the once highly unpopular secondary moderns, or dare imply some children are simply not worth educating properly. No mainstream political grouping, bar UKIP, argues for the return of the grammars. The shared educational credo of most political parties in the early twenty-first century is that every child, regardless of background, should be given access to the widest range of knowledge to the highest standard. That credo is a testament to the success of comprehensive education.

The challenge for the immediate future, then, is of a different order. It is not to reverse the comprehensive revolution but to consolidate, and further improve upon it. The battleground has shifted, and many of the fresh threats and barriers to a high quality comprehensive system lie elsewhere. Some argue that the real problem with state schools lies not in the non-selective principle but with the notion of 'progressive education'. Others aver that only privatisation and the creation of a market-based system of schooling will bring about a good state system. New myths have sprung up as part of these new campaigns – fresh worries planted in the public mind, in order to further chip away at confidence in state education. It is to one of the most enduring and unfounded of these untruths that we must now turn.

Notes

1 http://www.telegraph.co.uk/education/educationnews/8493158/Schoolchildren-being-failed-by-comprehensive-education.html accessed 28 January 2015.
2 http://www.dailymail.co.uk/news/article-377445/Comprehensive-schools-failing-poor-pupils.html accessed 28 January 2015.
3 http://www.theguardian.com/commentisfree/2013/jan/04/comprehensive-schools-failed-working-class accessed 28 January 2015.

Comprehensive education has failed

4 http://hitchensblog.mailonsunday.co.uk/2014/03/what-about-the-conmprehensive-failures.html accessed 28 January 2015.
5 From the introduction to http://www.policyexchange.org.uk/images/publications/choice%20what%20choice%20-%20nov%2007.pdf accessed 28 January 2015.
6 Robert Peal, *Progressively worse: The burden of bad ideas in British schools*, Civitas, 2014, p. 49.
7 http://www.independent.co.uk/news/education/education-news/grammar-schools-widen-gap-between-rich-and-poor-9449702.html accessed 28 January 2015.
8 http://www.independent.co.uk/news/education/education-news/grammar-schools-widen-gap-between-rich-and-poor-9449702.html accessed 28 January 2015.
9 John-Paul Flintoff, *Comp: A survivor's tale*, London: Victor Gollancz, 1998.
10 Tony Blair, *A journey: My political life*, New York: Alfred A. Knopf, 2010, p. 579.
11 Peter Hitchens *Mail on Sunday* September 2011 http://hitchensblog.mailonsunday.co.uk/2011/09/why-i-hope-free-schools-fail.html accessed 28 January 2015.
12 http://www.gq-magazine.co.uk/comment/articles/2010-10/11/gq-comment-tony-parsons-state-private-grammar-schools-education accessed 28 January 2015.
13 Diane Ravitch, *Reign of error*, New York: Alfred Knopf, 2013, p. 4.
14 http://www.oecd.org/education/school/50293148.pdf accessed 28 January 2015 (paragraph 2 Executive Summary – note: 'upper secondary' in this context is 16+).
15 http://www.independent.co.uk/news/education/education-news/grammar-schools-widen-gap-between-rich-and-poor-9449702.html accessed 28 January 2015.
16 http://theconversation.com/hard-evidence-do-grammar-schools-boost-social-mobility-28121 accessed 28 January 2015.
17 Richard Alleyne, '11-plus failure that still hurts 50 years later', *Daily Telegraph* http://www.telegraph.co.uk/news/uknews/1505898/11-plus-failure-that-still-hurts-50-years-later.html accessed 28 January 2015.
18 Graeme Paton, 'Adults "put off education for life" after failing 11-plus', *Daily Telegraph* http://www.telegraph.co.uk/education/educationnews/9547771/Adults-put-off-education-for-life-after-failing-11-plus.html accessed 28 January 2015.
19 Ross McKibben, *Classes and cultures: England 1918-1951*, Oxford: Oxford University Press, 2000, p. 262.
20 See the Gurney-Dixon Report (1954) Early Leaving Central Advisory Council for Education. To understand the human story behind such statistics, see also Alan Johnson, *This boy: A memoir of a childhood*, Corgi, 2014.

Comprehensive education has failed

21 Adrian Elliott, *State schools in the 1950s: The good news*, London: Trentham Books, 2007, p. 50.

22 Simon Jenkins, 'Cameron's historic victory over the gilded myth of grammars', *Sunday Times*, 27 May 2007.

23 Education: Historical statistics, Standard Note: SN/SG/4252, November 2012, Author: Paul Bolton, House of Commons Library, www.parliament.uk/briefing-papers/sn04252.pdf accessed 28 January 2015.

24 Brian Simon, *What future for education?*, London: Lawrence and Wishart, 1992, p. 76.

25 Education: Historical statistics, Standard Note: SN/SG/4252, November 2012, Author: Paul Bolton, House of Commons Library, www.parliament.uk/briefing-papers/sn04252.pdf accessed 28 January 2015.

26 Selina Todd, *The people: The rise and fall of the working class*, London: John Murray, p. 278.

27 Chris Cook, 'Grammar School Myths', *Financial Times*, 28 January 2013. http://blogs.ft.com/ftdata/2013/01/28/grammar-school-myths/ accessed 28 January 2015.

28 Anusha Asthana, 'Early starts for the children desperate to pass their 11-plus', *The Observer*, 11 October 2009 http://www.guardian.co.uk/education/2009/oct/11/grammar-schools-tuition-private-tutor accessed 28 January 2015.

29 Irena Barker, 'Does "tutor-proof" 11-plus let down the disadvantaged?', *Times Educational Supplement*, 5 December 2014.

30 Lucy Cavendish, 'The 11-plus has taken over my life', *Daily Telegraph*, 18 January 2011 http://www.telegraph.co.uk/education/8264590/The-11-plus-has-taken-over-my-life.html accessed 28 January 2015.

31 For a good example of this sort of locally based success in a deprived London borough, see Alan Boyle and Salli Humphreys, *A revolution in a decade: Ten out of ten*, London: Leannta publishing, 2012.

32 http://selinatodd.com/essays-and-jottings/ accessed 28 January 2015.

33 The Annual Report of Her Majesty's Chief Inspector of Education, Children's Services and Skills 2010/11http://www.ofsted.gov.uk/resources/annualreport1011 accessed 28 January 2015. The 2012 Ofsted Annual Report did not quote the figure for parental approval.

34 Education Act 2002 Section 482(2)(a) and(b).

35 http://www.theguardian.com/education/2013/dec/14/ofsted-chief-war-grammar-schools accessed 28 January 2015.

36 http://samfreedman1.blogspot.co.uk accessed 28 January 2015.

37 http://www.prospectmagazine.co.uk/magazine/the-social-mobility-myth-education-philip-colllins/#.U3XjmuDw6QK accessed 28 January 2015.

38 Cited in https://www.spi.ox.ac.uk/fileadmin/documents/PDF/Goldthorpe_Social_Mob_paper_01.pdf accessed 28 January 2015.

39 http://www.suttontrust.com/our-work/research/item/intergenerational-mobility-in-europe-and-north-america/ accessed 28 January 2015.

40 http://www.prospectmagazine.co.uk/magazine/the-social-mobility-myth-education-philip-colllins/#.U3XjmuDw6QK accessed 28 January 2015.

41 https://www.spi.ox.ac.uk/fileadmin/documents/PDF/Goldthorpe_Social_Mob_paper_01.pdf accessed 28 January 2015.

42 http://www.prospectmagazine.co.uk/magazine/the-social-mobility-myth-education-philip-colllins/#.U3TpNeDw6QJ accessed 28 January 2015.

43 Bernard Barker and Kate Hoskins, *Education and social mobility*, London: Trentham Books, 2014.

44 http://socialisteducationalassociation.org/2014/11/12/caroline-benn-memorial-lecture-busting-grammar-school-myths/ accessed 28 January 2015.

45 *Unlocking the Gate*: Barnardo's report into School Admissions, 2010 http://www.barnardos.org.uk/unlocking_the_gates-2.pdf accessed 28 January 2015.

46 http://skills.oecd.org/OECD_Skills_Outlook_2013.pdf accessed 28 January 2015.

47 http://www.tes.co.uk/article.aspx?storycode=6387517 accessed 28 January 2015.

48 http://www.ted.com/talks/andreas_schleicher_use_data_to_build_better_schools.html accessed 28 January 2015.

49 http://www.dailymail.co.uk/debate/article-2573444/SARAH-VINE-Why-Ive-chosen-send-daughter-state-school.html accessed 28 January 2015.

Local authorities control and hold back schools

Of all the myths under consideration here, the idea that local authorities 'control' schools is by far the simplest, and by far the most repeated. It is an accusation frequently levelled by those who want to eliminate the role of local authorities entirely in education and replace them with 'diverse providers', including academy chains and other groups of schools (see Chapters 3 and 4 for further discussion of this development).

Indeed, those who hold this view now even go so far as to argue that local authority involvement in education is best considered as an historical anomaly: a prolonged period of statist interruption of, and interference in, more diverse and autonomous local arrangements for education. According to James O'Shaughnessy, a former adviser on education to Prime Minister David Cameron, 'the period of municipalised control of schools in the twentieth century, which began in earnest with the 1902 Education Act and became dominant after the Second World War, is the historical aberration'. It was, O'Shaughnessy suggests,

> the point where the pendulum swung towards *state control*. New local education authorities covered the whole country, no longer simply filling in the gaps,

and they took responsibility not only for education in those schools provided on the rates . . . It marked the beginning of the end of the pluralist system . . . . with the 1944 Act secured finally ensuring *the dominance of local authorities* in controlling comprehensive education in every area . . . . This municipalisation of schools was largely the result of *government mission creep*.[1] (our emphasis)

Note the use of language, deliberately conjuring up images of soviet-style domination. In fact, as many knowledgeable commentators across the political spectrum observe, the role and performance of local authorities has always been more complex and diverse than this simplistic, hostile caricature allows. Some have provided excellent support to their local 'family' of schools while others have struggled, for a variety of reasons, to offer the appropriate provision and backing to schools in their locality.[2] And far from working to strengthen local performance where it is weak, successive governments have instead increased and bolstered state power from the centre. One of the most important, if under-stated developments in education in this country since 1988 has been the steady accretion of powers by central government, largely at the expense of local government'.[3]

Despite this, implacable political opponents of the role of local government in education have stuck to this one note theme of local 'control'. The frequently declared aim of former Secretary of State for Education Michael Gove was 'to liberate comprehensives from the dead hand of town hall control'. Instead they were to become part of academy chains.[4] (For more on how the chains are working see Chapter 5.) Writing in the *Daily Telegraph* in the summer of 2014 Mathew D'Ancona argued that in promoting his reforms Michael Gove 'sought to liberate comprehensives from the dead hand of town hall control'.[5] Nick Gibb, during his first tenure as Schools Minister in 2011 described the proscribed duties of local government as 'local authority meddling'.[6] Toby Young, blogging in *The telegraph*, said they represented the 'dead hand of local authority control'.[7] It is common for the Department for Education (DfE) to repeat the claim that academies have more autonomy than other schools because they are not under the 'control' of local authorities and even more common for the press to echo this claim, as if this is undisputed fact.[8]

Some clarifications and corrections are urgently required in relation to the true role of local authorities, and the balance between central and local government in the current landscape. We will begin by looking at five reasons why local authorities do not control maintained schools but central government attempts to do so.

First: maintained schools have control over their budgets

Local Management of Schools (LMS), introduced in the Education Reform Act 1988, gave schools control of most of their budget. Financial and staffing responsibilities were delegated to school governing bodies. The theory, and practice, behind LMS is that it enables a headteacher and the school's governing body to use better the school's human and financial resources than could be done by an inevitably more distant local authority. The school is able to meet the educational needs and priorities of the community it serves as it is much closer to it.

Local authorities continue to provide services to schools, such as payroll, most school improvement support and governance support, but this is on a payback basis and schools are free to go elsewhere. This is also true of academy chains except that academy chains can force academies to use central services provided by the chain. The local authority does manage a few services on

24

behalf of schools such as provision for special educational needs but this is done in collaboration with schools through the schools forum, made up of representatives of schools and the local authority.

Academies and free schools receive their entire allocated budget directly from the government. Academies, or when in a chain, the chain, are free to purchase the management and other services they need. There is little supervision from the government except through the hideously complicated funding agreement and articles of association. The rules are frequently being broken with examples coming to light about how academy chain trustees have been able to let contracts to their friends' and own companies.[9] The likelihood is that the rules will be tightened and central government will gain powers over how academies spend their money which local authority maintained schools have not seen for 25 years.

Local authorities do not tell schools how to spend their budget. Neither do they provide 'matched funding' in order to persuade schools to purchase resources from a restricted list as the DfE did with its matched funding[10] for synthetic phonics materials. Nor do local authorities promote materials closely associated to a schools minister. But this is exactly what happened when former Education Secretary Michael Gove and Schools Minister Elizabeth Truss praised E. D. Hirsch's Core Curriculum.

The story goes like this. The UK version[11] of the so-called core curriculum was rewritten for this country by Annaliese Briggs, the short-lived head[12] of Pimlico Primary Free School, a free school that is part of the Future Academies Trust set up by Tory donor John, now Lord, Nash before he was fast-tracked to the peerage in order to become Schools Minister in the Lords. (Briggs herself now works for Policy Exchange, the think tank founded by Michael Gove.) Lord Nash set up The Curriculum Centre (TCC) with his wife to disseminate the

Core Curriculum.[13] The TCC acts as Curriculum Director of Studies in Future Academies Trust schools and oversees the content of what is taught in all its academies. A series of books[14] based on the Core Curriculum marketed at parents and educators is published by right-leaning think tank Civitas. They are promoted as showing what a 'good' curriculum looks like. ConservativeHome claims 'lessons learned' by The New Model School Company Ltd, an offshoot of Civitas, were 'an important influence' on Michael Gove MP, then shadow schools secretary, as he was drafting 'a supply-side revolution for the whole of the UK schools system' in 2009.[15] This web connecting ministers, a preferred curriculum, educational publications, a think tank, an academy chain and educational policy is more complicated and wide-reaching than anything ever attempted by local authorities.

Second: local authorities do not tell schools what and how to teach

Local authorities do not tell schools what and how to teach. We have seen how ministers promote materials which chime with their ideas. But that is not the only way the DfE attempts to control what schools teach. In recent years it has been the DfE, not local authorities, which has increasingly forced on schools its ideas of what should be taught by imposing a National Curriculum.

In theory, this curriculum does not apply to academies and free schools. In practice, 'freedom from the National Curriculum is somewhat illusory when Ofsted are likely to judge us on it' as one academy head said to a survey about what motivated schools to convert to academies.[16] Only 1.8 per cent of heads chose opting out of the National Curriculum as the main motive for conversion.

Despite this compulsion to follow the National Curriculum, the report found two fifths (39 per cent) of academies believed it already allowed them sufficient freedom to innovate without the need to convert. And in 2008 when Labour was in power, Conor Ryan, who had been David Blunkett's special adviser at the Department for Education and Employment from 1997–2001, admitted that 'other [i.e. non-academy] state-funded schools have more curriculum and pay flexibility than [academies] use'.[17] In other words, non-academies had freedom to change the curriculum or teacher pay but, in Ryan's opinion, were not using it to the fullest extent.

Yet, despite the evidence, the DfE insists that academy status allows more room to innovate because it frees schools from local authority 'control'. The Academies Commission found it wasn't local authorities which stifled innovation but league tables. It wrote it had 'heard considerable evidence that the current accountability framework inhibits change and innovation'.[18] And the accountability system is decided by the DfE not by local authorities.

It has been ministers, not local authorities, who have laid down how teachers should teach. Ofsted is now charged with commenting on primary schools' use of phonics, thereby interfering with teachers' professional judgement if they should wish to teach reading using other methods or a combination of methods. Pupils taking Key Stage 2 maths SATs will no longer be rewarded for using a method such as chunking which Education Minister Nick Gibb, described as 'discredited'.[19] Former Schools Minister Elizabeth Truss dismissed the grid method of multiplication because she claims such strategies 'are not quick, efficient methods, nor are they methods children can build on and apply to more complicated problems'.[20] But this method can be applied to algebraic problems. Nevertheless, the minister has decreed that no marks for method will be awarded to any child using the grid method in maths SATs.

Local authorities control and hold back schools

It is not local authorities who lay down – or ban – particular methods of teaching, it is ministers basing the education system on their own views and prejudices and academy chains enforcing the mandatory use of particular materials or methods. Academy chains and central government apply more control over what is taught than ever local authorities did.

Academy chains can impose particular resources or methods of teaching onto their academies. For example, the Learning Schools Trust operates academies in England on behalf of Kunskapsskolan, a Swedish for-profit education provider.[21] LST academies use 'Kunskapsskolan's unique personalised learning model'. Ofsted judged two of LST's three sponsored academies as 'Requires Improvement' and one as 'Inadequate'. Ofsted criticised some aspects of the personalised learning programme which LST academies have to follow.[22] Learning Schools Trust was one of 14 academy chains restricted from sponsoring new academies or free schools following concerns about performance.[23]

Similarly – as described above – the Future Academies Trust uses the E. D. Hirsch-inspired core curriculum. This trust operates three of the four primary schools in Pimlico.[24] Such a monopoly raises the question about how genuinely autonomous the heads in future academies will be in terms of devising their own curriculum or how far they will be controlled by The Curriculum Centre which, as described above, works with Future Academies Trust to promote the Core Curriculum.

The Aurora Academies Trust charges its primary academies for their use of a patented 'Paragon curriculum'.[25] Payment goes to the Trust's US parent company. Ofsted has criticised the curriculum but heads in Aurora Academies Trust chain have no freedom to discard it. They can only tweak it to suit local circumstances.

No local authority mandates teaching curricula or materials in this way.

Third: local authorities cannot prevent free schools being established where there is no need

The DfE can override local opposition to the establishment of a free school. In Beccles where the Conservative leader of the council and the Conservative MP both feared the Beccles Free School would have a negative impact on the existing secondary school, the school went ahead anyway.[26] The National Audit Office 2013 found 81 per cent of secondary free schools had been set up in areas where there was already a surplus of school places.[27] Local authorities could not prevent this waste of taxpayers' money.

Fourth: local authorities cannot close an academy or free school due to falling demand

Only the Secretary of State can do this. At the same time, LAs cannot prevent a chain from closing an academy. Councillors in Lincolnshire were angry when West Grantham Academies Trust (WGAT) announced without consultation it would close one of its academies, Charles Read, in the village of Corby Glen. Lincolnshire County Council[28] was powerless to prevent closure and the school was only saved because the DfE handed it over to another academy chain.[29] The council, which had once advised all its schools to become academies belatedly realised that academisation made it difficult, if not impossible, to manage school place supply.[30]

Fifth: local authorities give their schools a great deal of freedom

This was one of the key findings of the Academies Commission: that local authority schools were not labouring

Local authorities control and hold back schools

under heavy-handed bureaucracy as the DfE claims. The OECD had already discovered this when it administered the 2009 PISA tests. It found the UK was among only four countries which gave schools a large amount of autonomy over using the budget, resource allocation and assessment.[31] But heads in academies could find themselves having less autonomy if they join an academy chain: the Academies Commission said academies in chains could result in less autonomy.[32] As we have seen above, academy chains can enforce curricula onto their schools. And they can also impose 'centrally mandated systems and practices', the Academies Commission found.[33]

In short, local authorities do not control schools. But central government attempts to do so. It does this by imposing curricula, either directly or indirectly by recommendation. Ministers decide which teaching methods are government-approved and ensure these are used either through Ofsted, or by refusing to award marks for particular methods in Key Stage 2 SATs, or promoting certain curricula in their speeches and mocking methods they dislike.[34] They have been accused of basing their education policies on their own prejudices and limited experience. In keeping with the new traditionalist position (see Chapter 7) former Schools Minister Elizabeth Truss disparaged what she dismissed as 'child-centred learning' and 'progressive education philosophy' because she scribbled over an Anti-Colouring Book when she was a child.[35] Former Schools Minister, Lord Baker, criticised former Secretary of State Michael Gove for using his own educational experience to inform his ideas.[36]

Michael Gove said academies were using their freedom from local authority 'control' to introduce 'Longer school days; better paid teachers; remedial classes; more personalised learning; improved discipline; innovative curricula'.[37]

But this claim was unfounded. The Academies Commission debunked it:

In short, many maintained schools have, in the words of the Secretary of State, introduced extended school days, remedial classes, more personalised learning, improved discipline and innovative curricula, to give their pupils the best possible education. In other words, most things an academy can do, a maintained school can also do.[38]

What, then, do local authorities do – and why are they vital for education? Below, we set out ten things that local authorities do, or provide, that directly improves the quality of education.

School places

Local authorities have a statutory duty to secure sufficient schools so that there is a place for every child in their area who needs one. Unfortunately, this is increasingly difficult to do because of the government's academies and free schools programme. Local authorities have no power to direct academies and free schools to expand to take extra children. Local authorities no longer have the ability to authorise the building of a new school – there is an assumption that any new provision will be either an academy or a free school. So local authorities have to tout around to find an academy chain or a free school group which will provide a new school and the DfE has to commission it. But the National Audit Office found the DfE had received no applications to open primary free schools in half of the areas where there is a high/severe need for extra places.[39]

Services

Local authorities offer a range of services to schools under their stewardship. These services are often offered to academies and free schools even though local authorities have no formal duty to do so. These might include every-thing from payroll for school staff, legal services, IT, property and contracts for school improvement services. Academies can choose whether to opt into these contracts if they don't want the legal and administrative burdens that come with managing such services themselves. The Academies Commission cited a National Audit Office report which found that nearly half of heads in academies felt less free from bureaucracy after conversion than they had been led to believe.[40]

Admissions

Local authorities co-ordinate admissions to all state schools in the area including free schools and academies.

Protection

Local authorities provide a protective umbrella to their schools. For example, Surrey County Council issued guid-ance for schools on how to produce an emergency plan with detailed instructions on who to contact for immediate help and advice.[41] Schools are able to use advice like this rather than devote resources to researching it themselves.

Support

Local authorities broker partnerships between schools particularly by matching a weaker school with a good or outstanding one. This collaboration was essential for the success of the London Challenge and similar initiatives. [42] Local authority brokerage services are not confined to local authority-maintained schools but can be accessed by academies. For example, an Ofsted monitoring inspec-tion of Batley Grammar School said, 'The local authority continues to give very good support despite having no formal responsibility for the Free School. The local authority is funding a secondary school improvement partner and both staff and governors benefit from local authority training events.'[43]

Accountability

Local authorities have a statutory duty to hold schools to account in their area and intervene if performance isn't good enough. In practice, however, this can be difficult if academy schools don't want to cooperate.

Nevertheless, local authorities continue to support their schools. For example, Ofsted wrote this about Peterborough's school improvement service after an inspection triggered by concerns about performance of children in the city: 'The local authority's senior leaders and the team of school improvement advisers are held in high regard by schools. They work well with local leaders of education and head teachers to support schools that are causing concern.'[44]

And a Lincolnshire primary school, Bourne Westfield Primary Academy, whose Ofsted judgement rose from Requires Improvement to Outstanding in June 2014, told inspectors the academy continued to buy in 'highly valued' local authority services including training.[45]

Auditing accounts

Accounts in local authority schools are publicly audited. Their accounts are subjected to effective scrutiny and auditors are obliged to make public any concerns they find.[46] This contrasts with academies and free schools whose accounts are audited by a private auditor employed by the academy/free school trust. Audited academy accounts must be sent to the Education Funding Agency (EFA) but the National Audit Office (2013) found that one-fifth of 435 academy trusts with audited accounts from 2010/11 did not return them to the Young Person's Learning Agency (the predecessor to the EFA) by the deadline.[47]

In January 2014, the NAO identified risks in the DfE's ability to manage academy finances.[48] As a result, the auditor 'qualified' the accounts for the whole Department as the Controller and Auditor General (CAG) had reservations arising from these concerns.[49] The DfE has put in place procedures to manage these risks but doubts remain over the EFA's ability to oversee the accounts of thousands of academies as their numbers rise. Local authorities have far fewer schools to audit and are therefore better placed to spot financial irregularities. They are also obliged by law to make such concerns public.

By law, local authorities have to ensure there is an adequate and effective internal audit under the 1996 Accounts and Audit Regulations. Accounts in local authority schools form part of each local authority's overall accounting arrangements and are covered by the same internal and external audit arrangements applying to the local authority as a whole.

Special needs

Local authorities have a statutory duty for children with special educational needs and disabilities. They carry out assessments[50] and issue Education, Health and Care plans which specify a child's needs and would name the school which the parent wishes the child to attend.[51] Until recently, academies could appeal to the Secretary of State to make a different determination, a loophole in the law now closed after the Academies Commission found the implications of this baffled even legal experts.[52]

Welfare

Local authorities also provide Education Welfare Services. For example, Leicester Educational Welfare Service is responsible for such things as school attendance, child employment, home education and chaperone services.[53]

Pupil and parent champions

Local authorities have responsibility for managing Fair Access Protocols for hard-to-place children. Unfortunately, this is sometimes hampered by the academies programme. A combined report by the Local Government Association (LGA) and the DfE found local authorities feared that academy conversion could lead to schools refusing to take their fair share of such children.[54] The report also found that although many local authorities were confident about their ability to commission support for vulnerable children, there was concern about any instability caused by providers (especially of alternative provision) entering and leaving the market rapidly.

Above all, local authorities can act as champions for pupils and parents. The combined LGA/DFE report advised learning from best practice such as the expertise of the Children's Improvement Board (CIB) which was set up in 2011 as a sector-led initiative to help LAs improve performance on adoption, tackling child sexual exploitation and learning lessons from child abuse cases. But the government axed funding for CIB with no notice in 2013.[55] This is just one part of a deliberate strategy to further reduce local authorities' capacity to deliver their statutory duties and to improve themselves. It appears Michael Gove was attempting to destabilise and deconstruct the local authority infrastructure.

As we have already pointed out, local authorities play a crucial role in school improvement. They know local schools well and can intervene early (and long before Ofsted gets round to visiting) to provide both support and challenge. However, their power to intervene in struggling converter academies is limited. Labour's 'Putting Students and Parents First' describes how one local authority met with DfE officials in March 2013 to express concern about the standard of education at a converter academy but the DfE failed to act until the LA made a second complaint. This example, the report said, 'indicates the peril a school must find itself in before a vastly cut-down Department will act'.[56]

So we can lay another key myth to rest. Instead of local authorities exerting heavy-handed 'control' they offer vital services, many of which they are required to do by law. Contrary to the argument put by James O'Shaughnessy, quoted earlier, local authority involvement in education has, on the whole, worked well – until, that is, central government began to assert its own imperious power and, post austerity, to cut back radically on local budgets. As Peter Mortimore argues, 'for nearly 100 years before ministers began to usurp their powers . . . England [had] a good tradition of central–local government partnerships'. Mortimore quotes former government minister, George Tomlinson, on how a genuinely

> progressive partnership of this kind [allows the creation of] a single, but not uniform, system out of many diverse elements; to widen educational opportunity and, at the same time, to raise standards; to knit the educational system more closely into the life of [a] community.[57]

Sadly, however, the possibilities of such a partnership, progressive or otherwise, have been consistently undermined by successive governments. In many areas, local authorities are being replaced by a patchwork of provision, including academy chains, that, as we have shown, have the potential to be far more 'controlling'. David Blunkett, neatly summarised this irony:

Local authorities control and hold back schools

The worst chains are replicating the worst of what people said local authorities were doing—top-down, emphasis on outside rather than inside improvement of the school, taking away the autonomy of school heads to manage, recruit and be a driving force.[58]

Speaking in early 2015, Tristram Hunt, Labour shadow spokesman on education argued that 'I see far more control, micro-managing and revenue-skimming [in academy chains] than in many a local authority'.[59]

The widespread failure of the academy chains (see Chapter 5) bolsters alternative arguments concerning the most effective, accountable school organisation for the future. Far from undercutting local authorities, many now argue that we need to reinvent, and improve, local means of collaboration, support and participation. In his report, 'Putting Students and Parents First', former Secretary of State for Education David Blunkett outlined plans for a new form of local oversight. He proposed 'an end . . . to [the] centralisation of powers in education [and instead] provide local oversight, support and challenge for all schools with a new Director of School Standards overseeing school improvement in local areas'.[60] The proposed DSS would not return powers to single local authorities but would create a new supra-regional structure to oversee schools and manage decisions, for example on school places, within groups of local authorities.

Opinion was divided on the plan. In a recent discussion on the Local Schools Network of how the 'middle tier' should develop in the coming years, Fiona Millar argues in favour of the DSS plan on the grounds that 'in politics it is always easier to go forward and create something new than it is to re-create the past'.[61] Others believe that local authorities continue to be the most effective administrative unit within which to organise education. As Henry Stewart argues,

Local authorities control and hold back schools

> Let's face reality. Local authorities are always going to be part of the solution . . . Where do [parents] go when things go wrong? . . . They overwhelmingly go to their council and [even if they didn't bother to vote] to their local councillor. Call me old-fashioned but that good old democratic accountability is something to support and enhance, not disregard in a new combination of centralisation and atomisation.[62]

Many point to the success of London boroughs like Tower Hamlets and Hackney, the latter once seen as one of the worst-performing boroughs in the country. Intervention by the Learning Trust (an arms-length, not-for-profit organisation) helped turn Hackney schools around, eventually enabling the local authority to once more take over responsibility for education in the borough; it now acts as central broker of everything from school improvement strategies to fair admissions. As the authors of a study of Hackney's (continuing) success concluded, 'In order to tackle disadvantage more systematically we need to look at *high-performing education systems* in deprived areas *rather than individual schools*' (our emphasis).[63] Alan Wood, director of children's services in Hackney, says: 'A partnership of local authority, parents and schools can work together to embrace a diversity of autonomous schools, including academies, and still raise standards for children and young people in our communities'.[64] Hackney works across all school types, and embraces both academies and maintained schools, at primary and secondary level.

It is such a detailed knowledge of the local scene, building a sense of relationship between different institutions and helping them to learn from each other that makes the local authority dimension so important. At its best, it is everything to do with support, and nothing to do with control.

Notes

1 J. O'Shaughnessy, 'Competition Meets Collaboration: helping school chains address England's long tail of educational failure', *Policy Exchange Report*, 2012, p. 16.

2 For two contrasting views of the role of local authorities in recent decades, see Andrew Adonis *Education, education, education: Reforming England's schools*, Biteback Publishing, 2012, and Peter Mortimore, *Education under siege: Why there is a better alternative*, Policy Press, 2013.

3 Peter Mortimore, *Education under siege: Why there is a better alternative*, Policy Press, 2013, p. 202. Also, see lecture by Professor Tim Brighouse to the Oxford Education Society, on May 16th 2011, 'Decline and fall: are state schools and universities on the point of collapse?'.

4 http://www.localschoolsnetwork.org.uk/2015/03/dfe-reveals-dismal-performance-of-academy-chains/ accessed 28 January 2015.

5 http://www.telegraph.co.uk/education/educationopinion/11038125/Does-the-passion-of-Michael-Gove-still-burn-bright.html accessed 28 January 2015.

6 http://www.conservativehome.com/platform/2011/11/nick-gibb-mp-the-education-act-will-help-free-teachers-from-bureaucracy-and-restore-discipline-to-cl.html accessed 28 January 2015.

7 http://blogs.telegraph.co.uk/news/tobyyoung/100280038/cabinet-reshuffle-has-michael-gove-been-eaten-by-the-blob/ accessed 28 January 2015.

8 http://www.education.gov.uk/schools/leadership/typesofschools/academies/b00205692/whatisanacademy accessed 28 January 2015.

9 http://www.parliament.uk/documents/commons-committees/Education/Conflicts-of-interest-in-academies-report.pdf accessed 28 January 2015. See page 16 for example.

10 https://www.gov.uk/government/news/funding-for-phonics-teaching-to-improve-childrens-reading (the scheme ended in Autumn 2013) accessed 28 January 2015.

11 http://www.coreknowledge.org.uk/ckuk.php accessed 28 January 2015.

12 http://www.bbc.co.uk/news/uk-england-london-24466928 accessed 28 January 2015.

13 http://www.thecurriculumcentre.org/ accessed 28 January 2015.

14 http://www.civitas.org.uk/shop.php accessed 28 January 2015.

15 http://conservativehome.blogs.com/thinktankcentral/2009/12/profile-of-civitas.html accessed 28 January 2015.

16 http://www.reform.co.uk/wp-content/uploads/2014/10/Plan_A_FINAL-1.pdf accessed 28 January 2015.

17 http://www.progressonline.org.uk/2008/07/23/a-growing-consensus/ accessed 28 January 2015.

Local authorities control and hold back schools

18 http://www.thersa.org/_ _data/assets/pdf_file/0020/1008038/ Unleashing-greatness.pdf (p. 30) accessed 28 January 2015.
19 http://www.publications.parliament.uk/pa/cm201314/cmhansrd/ cm140106/debtext/140106-0001.htm#1401066000006 accessed 28 January 2015.
20 http://www.tes.co.uk/article.aspx?storycode=6389538#sthash.7O DMm8cT.dpuf accessed 28 January 2015.
21 http://www.learningschoolstrust.org.uk/ accessed 28 January 2015.
22 Ofsted reports for the three LST academies, Ipswich Academy, Twickenham Academy and Hampton Academy can be downloaded here: http://reports.ofsted.gov.uk/ accessed 28 January 2015.
23 http://www.publications.parliament.uk/pa/cm201314/cmhansrd/ cm140318/text/140318w0002.htm#140318w0002.htm_spnew53 accessed 28 January 2015.
24 http://www.westendextra.com/news/2013/oct/facing-facts-teaching-fears-pimlico-primary-school-parents-%E2%80%98left-very-little-choice%E2%80%99 accessed 28 January 2015.
25 http://www.theguardian.com/education/2013/may/18/academy-pays-for-us-curriculum accessed 28 January 2015.
26 http://www.edp24.co.uk/news/waveney_mp_peter_aldous_and_ county_councillor_mark_bee_voice_disappointment_on_beccles_ free_school_decision_1_1389725 accessed 28 January 2015.
27 http://www.nao.org.uk/wp-content/uploads/2013/12/10314-001-Free-Schools-Book-Copy.pdf (p. 7) accessed 28 January 2015.
28 http://www.stamfordmercury.co.uk/news/education/education-news/school-closure-decision-under-fire-from-council-1-4747377 accessed 28 January 2015.
29 http://www.stamfordmercury.co.uk/news/education/education-news/charles-read-academy-saved-from-closure-by-trust-1-5181862 accessed 28 January 2015.
30 http://www.stamfordmercury.co.uk/news/education/education-news/lincolnshire-county-council-tells-schools-to-become-academies-and-make-their-own-rules-1-3041539 accessed 28 January 2015.
31 http://www.oecd.org/pisa/pisaproducts/pisainfocus/48910490.pdf accessed 28 January 2015.
32 http://www.thersa.org/_ _data/assets/pdf_file/0020/1008038/ Unleashing-greatness.pdf (p. 50) accessed 28 January 2015.
33 Op. cit., p. 50.
34 http://www.localschoolsnetwork.org.uk/2013/05/middlemarch-misrepresentation-and-mr-men-another-gove-speech/accessed 28 January 2015.
35 https://www.gov.uk/government/speeches/elizabeth-truss-speaks-to-education-publishers-about-curriculum-reform accessed 28 January 2015.

Local authorities control and hold back schools

36 http://www.independent.co.uk/news/education/education-news/ michael-gove-criticised-by-lord-baker-for-policies-based-on-his-own-educational-experience-8902485.html accessed 28 January 2015.

37 https://www.gov.uk/government/speeches/michael-gove-speech-on-academies accessed 17 August 2015.

38 https://www.thersa.org/globalassets/pdfs/reports/unleashing-greatness.pdf (p. 47), accessed 17 August 2015.

39 http://schoolsimprovement.net/mixed-reactions-to-spending-watchdog-report-on-free-schools-programme/ accessed 28 January 2015.

40 http://www.thersa.org/__data/assets/pdf_file/0020/1008038/ Unleashing-greatness.pdf (p. 124) accessed 28 January 2015.

41 http://www.surreycc.gov.uk/__data/assets/pdf_file/0007/173383/ School-Emergency-Plan-GUIDANCE-V3.pdf accessed 28 January 2015.

42 http://webarchive.nationalarchives.gov.uk/20141124154759/ http://www.ofsted.gov.uk/resources/london-challenge accessed 28 January 2015.

43 downloadable from http://www.ofsted.gov.uk/inspection-reports/ find-inspection-report/provider/ELS/137487 accessed 28 January 2015.

44 Downloadable from http://www.ofsted.gov.uk/local-authorities/ peterborough accessed 28 January 2015.

45 http://reports.ofsted.gov.uk/inspection-reports/find-inspection-report/provider/ELS/137599 accessed 28 January 2015.

46 Bundred, Steve. School's out for Accountability, *Municipal Journal*, 12 February 2014, available to subscribers only accessed 28 January 2015.

47 http://www.nao.org.uk/wp-content/uploads/2013/03/010013-001-Academies-programme_with-correction-slip.pdf accessed 28 January 2015.

48 http://www.nao.org.uk/report/department-education-education-funding-agency-financial-statements-2012-13/ accessed 28 January 2015.

49 http://www.theguardian.com/education/2014/jan/16/academy-school-finances-nao-critical accessed 28 January 2015.

50 https://www.gov.uk/children-with-special-educational-needs/ assessments accessed 28 January 2015.

51 https://www.gov.uk/children-with-special-educational-needs/ statements accessed 28 January 2015.

52 http://www.thersa.org/__data/assets/pdf_file/0020/1008038/ Unleashing-greatness.pdf (p. 72) accessed 28 January 2015.

53 http://www.leicester.gov.uk/your-council-services/education-lifelong-learning/about-us/lea-services/welfare-service/ accessed 28 January 2015.

Local authorities control and hold back schools

54 http://moderngov.southwark.gov.uk/documents/s31369/ Local-authority-role-in-education-final-report-from-the-ISOS-Partnership.pdf accessed 28 January 2015.

55 http://www.cypnow.co.uk/cyp/news/1076872/dfe-axes-childrens-improvement-board-funding accessed 28 January 2015.

56 http://www.yourbritain.org.uk/uploads/editor/files/Putting_ Students_and_Parents_First.pdf accessed 28 January 2015.

57 Peter Mortimore, *Education under siege: Why there is a better alternative*, Policy Press, 2013, p. 203.

58 http://www.theguardian.com/education/2014/jul/02/david-blunkett-oversight-academies-schools accessed 28 January 2015.

59 He added that 'I see far more control, micro-managing and revenue-skimming than in many a local authority'.

60 http://www.yourbritain.org.uk/agenda-2015/policy-review/putting-students-and-parents-first accessed 28 January 2015.

61 http://www.localschoolsnetwork.org.uk/2014/06/who-and-what-is-in-the-middle-tier/ accessed 28 January 2015.

62 http://www.localschoolsnetwork.org.uk/2014/06/who-and-what-is-in-the-middle-tier/ accessed 28 January 2015.

63 Alan Boyle and Salli Humphreys, *A revolution in a decade: Ten out of ten*, Leannta publishing, 2012, p. 128.

64 http://www.theguardian.com/education/2011/jul/04/profit-making-academies accessed 28 January 2015.

Choice, competition and markets are the route to educational success

In recent years a powerful alliance of interest groups, governments, business and philanthropic capital have used their considerable political and financial influence to bring market-style solutions to the education systems of nations around the world. This has come to be known as the Global Education Reform Movement (GERM) and its approach is based on potent narrative: public education is 'broken' (see Chapter 1 for the UK version). Only competition, choice, standardisation of outcome and test-based accountability can fix it. This is perhaps the most seductive myth on offer in the current world of education – here and around the world. Leading US anti-corporate reformer Diane Ravitch sums it up pithily when she describes how pro-market reformers set out to prove that 'Traditional public [i.e. state] schools are bad; their supporters are apologists for the unions. [Meanwhile] those who advocate for charter schools, virtual schooling, and "school choice" are reformers; their supporters ... are championing the rights of minorities ... they are the leaders of the civil rights movement of our day'.[1]

Substitute 'free schools and academies' for 'charter schools' in Diane Ravitch's declaration and that is a fair representation of the debate now raging in the UK. Since the mid 1980s successive governments have progressively fallen prey to idea that 'choice and competition' will fix our 'broken' schools. A small number of 'independent state schools' were established in the late 1980s under a Tory government (city technology colleges) and in the early 2000s under New Labour (city academies) but the market experiment with our state education system went into overdrive with the election of the coalition government in 2010.

Free schools in Sweden and the charter school movement in the USA were hailed as bold experiments that had a lot to teach us. Within weeks, the coalition government pressed forward with widespread academisation and a relatively small, but highly influential and hugely costly, free school programme. With typical triumphalist rhetoric, Michael Gove told the Schools White Paper (2010) Select Committee, 'If you create, within a system, exemplar performers, that encourages innovation that others can emulate and helps standards improve in other areas as well.'[2]

At first, our system was to be fixed by 'new providers' working on a not-for-profit basis: a rainbow of charities, religious organisations, universities, philanthropically minded businesses and, increasingly, academy chains. But – as predicted by many – as more of the schools run on this not-for-profit basis face difficulties, further privatisation is urged as the only solution. Die-hard free market reformers rightly point out that most schools already procure a lot of private sector contracts, for building work, IT, HR and school improvement services, so why not go the whole hog and run schools directly for profit? Suddenly, for-profit schooling is the logical, the necessary, the urgent next step.[3] A Policy Exchange report, co-authored by the influential New Schools Network, written before 2010 argued that profit-making schools should be allowed; the Adam Smith Institute advised the government to allow profit-making schools in 2011; the Conservative think tank

BrightBlue advocated running schools for profit in early
2013.[4] Private papers drawn up by Michael Gove, made
public in summer 2013, revealed plans to convert academies and free schools into profit-making businesses 'using
hedge funds and venture capitalists' to raise money.[5]
Worldwide, the education market was estimated at $4.4
trillion in 2013 and is set to grow further by 2017. Many
organisations want a piece of this lucrative education pie.

Do independent state schools raise standards? We
will consider this question over the next three chapters,
beginning with an assessment of the global evidence.
Have new providers in Sweden and the US created better
schools? Do they produce a better educational model than
institutions they are supposed to 'outperform'? What has
the impact been of deregulation of the schools market, in
terms of everything from school building to teacher pay
and even school closure. Can it really be right, as Michael
Gove rather glibly claims, that 'Sometimes you need to say
"thank you and goodnight".'[6] And, finally, what of the new
potentially destructive element in the competitive arsenal –
performance-related pay (PRP) for teachers? Again, according to Michael Gove, PRP 'will give schools greater
flexibility to respond to specific conditions and reward
their best teachers'.[7] But does the international evidence
suggest that PRP motivates or demoralises?

The evidence on Sweden's free schools has gone from
mixed to pretty miserable. Early research appeared to
back the new schools. In 1997/8 a study by Sandström
and Bergström did find large positive gains but their
research has subsequently been criticised for its sample-
selection.[8] Ahlin (2003), also found a 'quite large positive'
effect when free schools were present. But these positive
results were only in maths, not in Swedish or English.[9]

A 2010 study by Böhlmark and Lindahl found a modest
increase in results for 15–16-year-olds when free schools
were in competition with state schools.[10] However, this

slight rise did not lead to long-term advantages. Pupils in areas with free schools were no more likely to achieve higher grades at 18/19 or at university than pupils from areas with no free schools. In 2012, Böhlmark and Lindahl concluded the programme had improved educational performance but that its lessons could not easily be transferred to other countries.[11]

But Rebecca Allen from the Institute of Education found those who benefited most from these schools were those from more privileged homes. 'The impact on low-educated families and immigrants is close to zero,' her report said. Echoing the Böhlmark and Lindahl study, it found

the advantages that children educated in areas with free schools have by age 16 do not translate into greater educational success in later life [. . .] The evidence on the impact of the reforms suggests that, so far, Swedish pupils do not appear to be harmed by the competition from private schools, but the new schools have not yet transformed educational attainment in Sweden.[12]

By late 2013, with the publication of PISA results, the shine had further come off Sweden's school revolution (and Michael Gove had already stopped referring to the Nordic country's reforms well before then). These results showed that Sweden's exam results had fallen abruptly across all three measures of reading, maths and science. The country recorded the largest drop in maths performance over 10 years. Then, in 2013, a major for-profit provider of free schools in Sweden, JB Education, filed for bankruptcy. According to a TES piece on the debacle,

The company's reputation had struggled to recover from a damning 2007 investigation by Sweden's TV4 channel, which revealed how its founder had become a millionaire despite the schools' many shortcomings.

Then, in June last year, Sweden's schools inspectorate issued a highly critical report of the group, putting nine of its schools under supervision.[13]

The business, owned by Axcel, a private equity firm, sustained heavy losses. The announcement to close schools was shambolic: the firm gave its principals just a few days' notice, its 10,000 pupils read about the bankruptcy in the media before being officially told by their schools and operators negotiating to take over some JB schools were furious when the news became public.

Putting the final nail in the Swedish free school coffin, Andreas Schleicher, Deputy Director for Education at the OECD, told the Education Select Committee in March 2014 that if you looked at how free schools operate in Sweden you might 'think twice'.[14]

What about the USA? Charter schools were originally set up as a way to improve, and individualise, the education of the most marginalised students in the American school system. In this early phase, the idea had the support of Albert Shanker, an influential teachers' union leader who later repudiated the reforms as he saw it as a vehicle for private takeover of public education. In subsequent years charter schools have become highly contentious as traditional public schools are threatened with closure, forced to share premises with the burgeoning privately-backed sector and teachers face redundancy if they do not meet certain agreed – and narrow – test standards.

But how well do charters actually perform? There have been two studies of Charter Schools carried out by Stanford University's Center for Research on Education Outcomes (CREDO). The first, in 2009, found that 17 per cent of schools did better than equivalent public sector schools, 46 per cent did the same (i.e. no statistically significant difference) and 37 per cent did worse. Overall, therefore, it did not seem that charters were outperforming equivalent public schools.[15]

The second CREDO Report, in 2013, split its analysis between reading and maths. In maths 29 per cent of charters did better and 31 per cent did worse (with 40 per cent about the same). In reading 25 per cent did better and 19 per cent did worse (with 56 per cent about the same). So at first glance charters did a little better in reading, slightly worse in maths. Again, being a charter school is clearly no guarantee of improvement.[16]

But the CREDO Report reveals something else: a major cause of improvement overall in charter schools from 2009 to 2013 was that the worst performing, 8 per cent of the total, were closed. Without that the performance would have been about the same in reading and clearly worse in maths.

So the one area of better performance in charter schools (in reading in the 2013 study) is explained not by issues such as greater autonomy but the fact they closed the ones that were doing poorly.

Since the publication of the CREDO Report, New York test results show charter schools did badly in exams aligned to Common Core State Standards.[17] Results were particularly poor at Knowledge Is Power Program (KIPP) charter schools, a charter within the charter movement that has attracted high praise from the liberal establishment – and UK government – for their tough 'no excuses' approach to learning. In a 2009 study W. Dobbie and R. Fryer found charter schools in Harlem Children Zone, New York, had had impressive results but writing in September 2012 Fryer said 'charter schools have yielded inconsistent results'.[18]

In a separate 2012 study, J. Angrist found positive results in a single KIPP charter school.[19] But Harvard University's Stephen Hoffman found the zero-tolerance behaviour model favoured by KIPP schools resulted in more black and ethnic minority pupils being excluded than in other schools. The effect was even worse when Hoffman studied the impact of the policy on pupils with special needs.[20]

Diane Ravitch now argues that the intensifying pressure on schools to get results – and in some cases, to make profits out of their students – is corrupting US education. Students that will harm test results are being turned away or excluded from charter schools and the curriculum of many has become degraded and thin. Teachers are put under intolerable pressure to get 'good scores' in standardised tests regardless of the intake of their class and are being punished for poor results.

According to Ravitch, three core principles are being ignored by the corporate reformers: first, that public education is a public good and that a broad and balanced curriculum should be on offer to all children, whatever their social and economic background; second, that a for-profit ethos in education means schools inevitably cut corners and deprive children of necessary resources and a rich experience; thirdly, that poverty clearly has a negative impact on many children's ability to learn and that politicians should concentrate on alleviating inequality rather than overload beleaguered teachers and hard-pressed students.

Laura McInerney points out two aspects of the American system that have direct relevance to the emerging UK experience. The American example shows the risk of exploitation of younger staff and teacher burnout. 'Given that time and money are precious many school leaders turn to young teachers whose energies are high but whose price is lower. One teacher on the board of a Charter School [described] how their school hired teachers in their early twenties because "they are less likely to have family obligations that would keep them from making the enormous time commitments necessary".'[21] Teacher burn-out becomes inevitable and contributes to the high numbers of teachers who leave the profession within five years: a problem that is already dogging the English school system.[22]

McInerney also points out one of the downsides of the 'new school' model that has particular application to England's free schools.

> The original US Charter Schools were encouraged to open in any available building. This led to schools opening in disused offices, warehouses, even shipping containers. At first this was seen as a realisation of American initiative and 'triumph over adversity'. But when unreliable contracts meant schools had to keep moving, or poor conditions led to poor health and high levels of staff absence, many schools suffered terribly. Without well-designed spaces, secured for long periods of time, the uncertainty took its toll on students and, particularly, on staff meaning these schools were the most likely to suffer high staff turnover and the associated damage to student relationships and achievement.[23]

The evidence from the USA on the success of performance-related pay is also not convincing. In a survey of several reports on the operation of the scheme in the US, Mehdi Hasan of the *Huffington Post* found scant evidence of success.[24] A 2010 US study published the results of a 'three-year experiment' involving 300 teachers; half of which were given bonuses worth up to 15,000 dollars a year, in a bid to improve their students performance in exams. At the end of the three years, both groups reported very similar results from their students. As the Vanderbilt study concluded: 'there was no overall effect on student achievement across the entire treatment group'.[25] In July 2011, a Rand Corporation study of a New York City programme that used increased pay to boost student performance found that overall, 'the program has no positive effects on student achievement at any grade level'. Interestingly the Rand study found: 'Other accountability incentives – such as receiving a high progress report grade or achieving adequate yearly progress targets – and intrinsic motivation were deemed by many teachers as more salient than financial rewards.'[26] And in 2012 the OECD concluded that 'A look at the overall picture reveals no relationship between average student performance in a country and the use of performance-based pay schemes'.[27]

According to the respected charity, the Education Endowment foundation, 'the actual average impact [of PRP] has been close to zero. In India, there is evidence of the benefit of performance pay in the private sector but not the state sector, but it is not clear how this evidence applies in the UK'. The EEF warned that 'Performance pay may lead to a narrower focus on test performance and restrict other aspects of learning'.[28]

The arguments of critics of corporate reform are echoed by the findings of two independent reviews of the evidence on the impact of market-style systems across the globe. A 2010 report for the OECD acknowledged that supporters of competition between schools believed it would result in 'higher quality, more efficiency and more demand sensitivity'. But they found the evidence that market mechanisms in education had a positive effect on outcomes was 'fragmented and often inconclusive' for a number of reasons.[29]

First, the scope of much research was limited and focused narrowly on test scores in reading and maths. This neglected other subjects and downgraded other kinds of achievement. Where positive effects had been found, these were small and limited to reading alone.

Second, 'the evidence provided by large-scale quantitative studies focusing on the impact of market mechanisms on student achievement is unstable among research methods, subjects, subgroups, contexts and research methods. If any conclusion is to be drawn, it might be that market mechanisms bear potentially positive effects, but even in cases where positive effects are found, they are very modest in size.'

Third, the reviewers expressed concern that more choice carried a risk of segregation between schools 'in terms of ethnic, socio-economic and ability segregation'. This was made worse, the reviewers said, when schools set out to attract certain types of children more than others – faith groups, for example, or more academic pupils. This kind of criticism has been levelled against both Swedish free schools and American charters whose opponents point out that they enrol far fewer special needs and minority students so creating additional problems for the public/state schools that cannot operate special admissions policies.[30,31]

In 'The Learning Curve', a special study of global educational data by Pearson and the Economic Intelligence Unit (EIU), published in 2012, the authors found there were no 'magic bullets' for raising educational standards.[32] The report said parental choice does not 'constitute a panacea' but tentatively suggested 'other research might point to the importance of school choice and school autonomy'. But the 'other research' was not all that it seemed.

'The Learning Curve' cited PISA 2003 which allegedly said the share of privately-managed schools had 'an economically and statistically significant positive effect on student achievement'. But this conclusion did not come from PISA as implied. It appeared in an academic paper co-authored by Ludger Woessmann, one of the academics interviewed for 'The Learning Curve'. Woessmann's research considered only 29 of the 40 countries that took part in PISA 2003 in the light of Catholic 'resistance' to state education.[33] What PISA 2003 actually said was:

> these [international] comparisons show that the association between a school being private and its students doing well is at best tenuous. Thus, any policy to enhance overall performance only by moving funding from public to private institutions is subject to considerable uncertainty.[34]

In other words, the evidence cited by 'The Learning Curve' said the exact opposite to the tentative claim made by the authors that increased choice raised school performance. PISA 2003 found no evidence that increasing parental choice by diverting money to private institutions increased overall achievement.

Nine years later, PISA 2012 repeated its conclusion about increased school choice. It tentatively suggested that its findings were 'consistent with [other] research showing that school choice—and, by extension, school competition—is related to greater levels of segregation in the school system which may have adverse consequences for equity in learning opportunities and outcomes'. PISA 2012 also found that 'System level correlations in PISA do *not* [author's emphasis] show a relationship between the degree of competition and student performance'.[35]

As for profit-making providers, the Institute for Public Policy Research (IPPR) published a report that reviewed the international evidence in this area. It showed that profit-making schools have not raised standards in Sweden compared to not-for-profit schools. It mainly referenced Sahlgren's work, but pointed to methodological problems in studies that don't control for school intake.[36]

Notes

1 Diane Ravitch, *Reign of error: The hoax of the privatisation movement and the danger to America's public schools*, New York: Alfred A. Knopf, 2013, p. 4.
2 http://www.publications.parliament.uk/pa/cm201011/cmselect/cmeduc/674/10121402.htm accessed 28 January 2015.
3 http://pasisahlberg.com/text-test/ accessed 28 January 2015.
4 http://www.independent.co.uk/news/uk/politics/cash-for-classrooms-michael-gove-plans-to-let-firms-run-schools-for-profit-8682395.html accessed 28 January 2015.
5 http://www.independent.co.uk/news/uk/politics/cash-for-classrooms-michael-gove-plans-to-let-firms-run-schools-for-profit-8682395.html accessed 28 January 2015.

Choice, competition and markets

6 http://www.bbc.co.uk/news/education-13393289 accessed 28 January 2015.
7 http://www.telegraph.co.uk/education/educationnews/9799356/Michael-Gove-to-confirm-plans-for-performance-related-pay-in-schools.html accessed 28 January 2015.
8 Rebecca Allen, *Replicating Swedish 'free school' reforms in England* http://www.bristol.ac.uk/cmpo/publications/allen10.pdf accessed 28 January 2015.
9 Allen, op. cit., p. 4.
10 Cited in http://www.llakes.org/wp-content/uploads/2010/09/Wiborg-online.pdf accessed 28 January 2015.
11 https://www.thersa.org/globalassets/pdfs/reports/unleashing-greatness.pdf accessed 28 January 2015.
12 http://www.bbc.co.uk/news/10376457 accessed 28 January 2015.
13 http://www.tes.co.uk/article.aspx?storycode=6341728 accessed 28 January 2015.
14 http://data.parliament.uk/writtenevidence/committeeevidence.svc/evidencedocument/education-committee/academies-and-free-schools/oral/7266.html accessed 28 January 2015.
15 *Multiple Choice: Charter School performance in 16 states*, Stanford University CREDO, 2009: http://bit.ly/09Credo1 accessed 28 January 2015.
16 *National Charter School Study 2013*, Stanford University CREDO: http://bit.ly/13Credo1 accessed 28 January 2015.
17 *Charters fail to make the grade* at http://www.tes.co.uk/article.aspx?storycode=6349163 accessed 28 January 2015.
18 http://scholar.harvard.edu/files/fryer/files/hamilton_project_paper_2012.pdf accessed 28 January 2015.
19 http://economics.mit.edu/files/5465 accessed 28 January 2015.
20 http://www.tes.co.uk/article.aspx?storycode=6343240 accessed 28 January 2015.
21 McInerney, op. cit.
22 http://www.publications.parliament.uk/pa/cm201012/cmselect/cmeduc/1515/151508.htm accessed 28 January 2015.
23 McInerney, op. cit.
24 http://www.huffingtonpost.co.uk/mehdi-hasan/performance-related-pay_b_4123357.html accessed 28 January 2015. The paragraphs that follow draw from Mehdi Hasan's piece; thanks to him.
25 http://news.vanderbilt.edu/2010/09/teacher-performance-pay/ accessed 28 January 2015.
26 http://www.rand.org/news/press/2011/07/18.html accessed 28 January 2015.
27 http://www.oecd.org/pisa/pisaproducts/pisainfocus/50328990.pdf accessed 28 January 2015.

Choice, competition and markets

28 http://educationendowmentfoundation.org.uk/toolkit/performance-pay/ accessed 28 January 2015.

29 http://www.oecd.org/officialdocuments/publicdisplaydocumentp df/?cote=EDU/WKP%282010%2915&docLanguage=En accessed 28 January 2015.

30 'Special education is emerging as their [the Charters'] Achilles' heel. Over the last few years, numerous reports have shown that most charters do not enrol as large a proportion of disabled children as do their traditional school counterparts.' Harvard Education Letter, Jan/Feb 2013, http://hepg.org/hel-home/issues/29_1/helarticle/making-charter-schools-more-inclusive_556 accessed 28 January 2015.

31 'Our findings suggest that charters currently isolate students by race and class . . . After two decades, the promise of charter schools to use choice to foster integration and equality in American education has not yet been realized'. *Choice without equity: charter school segregation*, Erica Frankenberg, Genevieve Siegel-Hawley, Jia Wang at http://epaa.asu.edu/ojs/article/view/779 accessed 28 January 2015.

32 http://thelearningcurve.pearson.com/reports/the-learning-curve-report-2012/executive-summary accessed 28 January 2015.

33 http://www.voxeu.org/article/competition-private-schools-boosts-performance-system-wide accessed 28 January 2015.

34 http://www.oecd.org/edu/school/programmeforinternational-studentassessmentpisa/34002454.pdf accessed 28 January 2015.

35 http://www.oecd.org/pisa/keyfindings/pisa-2012-results-volume-IV.pdf accessed 28 January 2015.

36 http://www.ippr.org/assets/media/images/media/files/publication/2012/08/not-for-profit-private-sector-englands-schools_Aug2012_9492.pdf accessed 28 January 2015.

Choice will improve education in England

The free school model

We have looked at the results of the choice, competition and marketisation in the international arena and seen the lack of clear evidence of its success. Despite this, supporters of this strategy in the UK continue to claim that the widespread imposition of free schools and academies has improved public education, and that these schools are not only offering more 'parent choice' but clearly outperforming existing provision in maintained schools. As Jenny Turner writes in the *London Review of Books*, 'The question is not whether education privatisation is going to happen. It is happening, but it looks different from what people were expecting. There's nothing grand or monolithic about it. It's uneven and piecemeal.'[1]

In the next chapter we test these claims in relation to academies, originally a model used to improve 'failing' state schools in deprived areas. However, academisation has been much more widely introduced, using a variety of centralised incentives and pressures, since 2010. Over half of England's secondary schools are now academies, although the rate of conversion is slowing down.[2]

But what of free schools? The particular 'selling point' of this model was that it would permit enthusiastic and creative groups of parents and teachers to set up their own schools and so bypass and outstrip existing poor state school provision. Since September 2011, 174 free schools have been opened; 24 in 2011, 55 in 2012 and 93 in September 2013. Another 116 were due to open in 2014.[3] Compared to the academy conversion programme, then, numbers have been relatively small but, given that these are schools started from scratch with the full weight of government behind them, 'free schools' remain a flagship policy. During the 2015 election campaign, despite mounting scepticism at the success of the programme, David Cameron promised that if the Conservatives won, he would continue with the policy and open 500 more free schools.

It is impossible to understate the hype that surrounded free schools when the idea was first launched. Here, we were told, was a model of non-selective local excellence that would be able to surmount, through sheer energy and enthusiasm, the multiple problems that dog so many existing schools. The Tory-dominated Coalition promised that parents would at last have a real choice as to where to send their children; standards would be high, and the competitive impact of a new school in the area would raise the standards of other schools.

Writing in 2010 when excitement around the model was at its height, writer and teacher Laura McInerney described how some free school founders often start out with a sense of 'feelings of superiority and uniqueness'. 'Many Free Schoolers think their goal *is* simple. Many have said to me they will "Help all pupils learn as best they can". Yet, this phrase means wildly different things across teachers and leaders.' She went on:

> many believed that their school would have none of the time or staffing constraints or problems within the community that existing local schools face. Filled with energy and enthusiasm, they will create a 'good' school

to replace a 'bad' school; their children will benefit from the individual attention that defines their mission as an 'alternative provider'.[4]

David Cameron took rather a similar line in 2012,

> Free schools symbolise everything that is good about the revolution that we are bringing to Britain's schools. Choice for parents, power in the hands of teachers, discipline and rigour and high quality education in areas that are crying out for more good local schools . . . Open up our schools to new providers and use the competition that results to drive up standards across the system. We are backing the parents, charities and committed teachers who are trying to make things better and giving them the freedoms they need to transform our education system.[5]

In the summer of 2013, Michael Gove confidently claimed that 'free schools were driving up standards across the board'.[6]

So how does the performance of free schools so far match the claims made for them? Has the model provided the vehicle for keen groups of local parents to create their own education provision? Has it met its initial promise to provide hundreds and thousands of much-needed school places a rapidly growing school population? And what of the general impact on the rest of the school landscape of the new competition offered by free schools and academies?

Let's begin with that claim made by Michael Gove in the summer of 2013 about free schools raising results. Given that only 24 schools had completed more than one full year of schooling and few had entered pupils for exams, it is difficult to discern how the results of this cohort had already driven 'standards up across the board' in such a short time. Of those 24, five, which had previously been independent schools, did enter pupils for tests but one school, the all-through Maharishi Free School did not follow Funding Agreement requirements and entered no pupils for Key Stage 2. Ofsted found three of the previously independent schools, Batley Grammar School, The Priors School and Sandbach School required improvement. Key Stage 2 results at the fifth previously independent school, Barnfield Moorland, dropped from 87 per cent reaching Level 4 or above in 2012 to 66 per cent in 2013. And Barnfield Federation, which ran the free school, was censured by the Education Funding Agency in 2014 for claiming £1m for non-existent students.[7]

Other claims have also proved equally flimsy. In November 2013, in a letter to a fellow peer, Schools Minister, Lord Nash, made the claim that Ofsted inspection results already proved that free schools 'outperform' local authority schools which had opened in the same period. In a letter to Baroness Jones of Whitchurch, Nash argued that 'half the local authority schools which had their first inspection under the new framework were rated good or outstanding, compared to three quarters of the first batch of free schools'. Lord Nash identified 16 such schools.[8]

A Freedom of Information request revealed that 20 mainstream community schools opened in September 2011.[9] However, 19 were a result of amalgamation; only one was new provision. It would be unreliable, therefore, to compare a sample of 24 free schools, five of which already existed, with an even smaller sample of 20 schools only one of which was new.

The beneficial effect of 'new school' competition has been claimed more recently. In March 2015 a Policy Exchange report entitled 'A Rising Tide' claimed that secondary schools closest to free schools perform 'better than . . . national average at secondary'. David Cameron quoted the report's 'findings' that same week, when he announced that any future Tory government would open 500 more free schools.

But the report's findings were flawed, according to analysis done by Henry Stewart for the Local Schools Network. Stewart found,

> If we discount those opening in 2011, where Policy Exchange accepts the sample is too small (just five schools), then there is virtually no difference between the change in results in schools close to free schools and those nationally. For 2012 and 2013 openers, the fall in GCSE results is exactly the same and for 2014 openers there is just a 1% difference . . . The argument for free schools is that they introduce competition that will improve the performance of all schools in the area. This is the basis of Cameron's argument and is the argument tested in the Policy Exchange document. However the data clearly does not support this. Overall the change in results of schools closest to a free school are remarkably similar to those nationally.[10]

The case for free schools was further damaged in early 2014, when it emerged that a number had fallen into difficulty on grounds of low quality or financial mismanagement. Discovery New School in West Sussex shut down at Easter 2014 after concerns about the quality of education on offer. Al Madinah in Derby is due to shut its secondary provision at the end of the summer term 2014 and criminal investigations continue into alleged financial mismanagement at the Kings Science Academy in Bradford. In 2011, *The Telegraph* had published a lengthy article about Sajid Raza (aka Sajid Hussain) the man who claimed to be leading the way in opening Kings Science Academy.[11] But in January 2013, Raza was arrested in connection with the alleged fraud and in August 2014 he was dismissed following a disciplinary investigation.[12] Raza, together with two former members of staff and Kings Science Academy, were charged with fraud in early 2015.[13] In a less well-publicised case, Hartsbrook E-Act free school was judged 'inadequate' in January 2014. Despite this ruling, the school continued to say it offered an 'outstanding' education on its website until Advertising Standards intervened.[14] Its sponsor, E-Act, was stripped of ten of its academies after Ofsted-focused inspections raised concerns about poor performance.[15] Hartsbrook E-Act closed in August 2014. Brook House Primary School, sponsored by Lion Academy Trust, opened in September in its place.[16]

Several high profile free schools have run into problems. In February 2014 Ofsted said Bedford Free School, whose head Mark Lehain was frequently lauded by Michael Gove, 'requires improvement'. Inspectors noted 'good leadership' but had concerns about some elements of the teaching. In March, IES Breckland, which is run by for-profit Swedish company IES, was put into Special Measures. In April, Greenwich Free School, another of the government's 'flagship' free schools, was judged to 'require improvement'. The school was co-founded by Jonathan Simons, head of education at the right-leaning think tank the Policy Exchange and Tom Shinner, Gove's senior policy adviser. It had been publicly praised by Gove for demonstrating that 'every child can succeed if given a classical liberal education'. Ofsted inspectors found the quality of teaching at Greenwich required improvement: too few students made good progress over all subjects, lower-ability students were falling behind in some lessons and disabled and special-needs students were not making the expected progress in Maths and English. In late 2014 Grindon Hall Christian School, a former independent school, and Durham Free School, were served with a Financial Notice to Improve. Both schools were judged Inadequate in January 2015 and DFS closed its doors at the end of March.

Such had been the worry within government in spring 2014 about the emerging problems in some free schools that the government prepared plans for a covert fast track scheme to help deal with troubled free schools before potentially damning, and public, Ofsted judgements. A 40-page document prepared for academies minister Lord Nash proposed that ministers monitor free schools through private education advisers and be responsible for making key early decisions on tackling problems because of the risk of major political fallout further down the road.[17]

In January 2015 the Education Select Committee agreed with Ofsted that it was 'too early to draw conclusions on the quality of education provided by free schools or their broader system impact'.[18]

When Michael Gove and David Cameron first mooted the idea of free schools, one of the major benefits of the policy was that it would provide a projected further 200,000 places. But with a policy based on random demand not planned need, this has not happened. According to a National Audit Office report in December 2013, 87 per cent of places in primary free schools are in areas of need but 81 per cent of secondary free school places are not. A third of these secondary school places are in London where there is no need for more places.[19] A quarter of free schools opened by September 2012 had 20 per cent fewer pupils than planned as did 47 per cent of free schools that opened in September 2012 and 38 per cent of free schools that opened in September 2013.[20] When the Public Accounts Committee expressed concern that there had been no requests to open free schools in some areas with a significant forecast need for additional school places, the Department confirmed that it had received no applications to open primary free schools from half of districts with a high or severe forecast need for extra school places – perhaps the clearest example of market weakness when it comes to provision of public services.[21]

Natalie Evans of the New Schools Network, the taxpayer-funded charity which promotes free schools, told the education journal TES that 'free schools are being set up in the communities that most need high-performing new schools – they are 10 times more likely to be in the most deprived parts of the country than the most affluent'.[22] But TES found these schools were not benefiting disadvantaged children – their intake had fewer pupils eligible for Pupil Premium, the extra funding given to children eligible for free school meals, than the average for their local area. For example, Canary Wharf College, a free school in Tower Hamlets, had just 4.4 per cent eligible for Pupil Premium. The Tower Hamlets average was 40.4 per cent. Similarly, West London Free School Primary, Hammersmith and Fulham, had just 6.7 per cent eligible for the premium. The average for the local area was 28.6 per cent.[23]

In May 2014 Michael Gove was accused of raiding £400m from the Basic Need fund for local authorities – a fund established in order to provide more school places. According to sources inside the coalition who leaked news of the minister's action, the money taken would help provide 30,000 new school places and would do much to ease pressure in areas where parents struggle to find places. Gove had taken the money to plug an £800m projected 'black hole' in spending on free schools between 2013 and 2016.[24] The angry coalition insider told *The Guardian*,

Everybody knows there's real pressure on school places at the moment and the secretary of state knows better than most. It is nothing short of lunacy to slash the amount of money available for new school places to lavish on free schools. The Conservatives are putting the needs of a handful of their pet projects ahead of the requirements of the other 24,000 schools in the country.[25]

Enabling market-style competition is a costly business – for the taxpayer. Free school costs are rising. Once again, the Public Accounts Committee registered concern at the capital costs of the programme:

> The Department's capital budget for free schools is £1.5 billion to March 2015, of which it estimates that it will have spent over £740 million by March 2014 since the launch of the programme in June 2010. The most recent round of approved free schools had a greater proportion of more expensive types, such as secondaries, special and alternative provision, located in more expensive regions such as London, the South East and South West. If this mix of approved free schools continues, there is a risk of costs exceeding available funding.[26]

A National Audit Office report noted that the Department for Education severely underestimated the total capital funding needed to set up free schools. Projected funding increased from £900m to £1.5bn, just over 8 per cent of the department's total capital budget. The average unit cost of premises is £6.6m: more than double the DfE's original estimates. The NAO also expressed concern about the rising capital cost of free schools versus unmet need for places pointing out that the estimated total capital costs for free schools opened in areas where there's no forecast need for extra school places are at least £241m out of a projected total of £950m for mainstream schools.[27] Updated Department of Education figures published in May 2014 also showed that government spent a total of £1,043,223 on free schools that were withdrawn in the pre-opening stage between 2011 and 2013.[28]

Given this background of concern, Gove acted with some audacity in his decision in March 2014 to give £45 million to a single London sixth form free school serving just 500 students. The projected Harris Westminster Sixth form 'for high-achieving students' cost six times the average of any other free school and the government subsidy came at a time when the country's sixth form colleges were facing unprecedented cuts worth £100 million over the past three years. Margaret Hodge, chair of the Public Accounts Committee, described the expenditure as 'outrageous ... This is nothing more than a vanity project that is taking precious resources away from areas which really need it in a time of austerity'. Her own Barking constituency is 'desperate for good quality school places for our children' yet Mr Gove's plans would only serve 'a tiny number of pupils ... I'm all for helping children from disadvantaged backgrounds ... but why does this school have to be in one of the most expensive areas of London?'[29]

A letter signed by 12 principals of sixth form colleges declared the minister's decision to be 'entirely unjust. Forty-five million pounds has been found to establish an institution that will educate less than a fifth of the number of students currently enrolled at some of the existing sixth form colleges in London while the total capital budget for all 93 sixth form colleges in England last year was less than £60m. Michael Gove has only succeeded in creating a fresh divide – between new, generously funded and often highly selective free school sixth forms and the very successful network of state sixth form colleges they are modelled on.'[30]

One of the subsidiary myths of the competition lobby is that providing new schools offered by diverse providers expands parental choice. Free schools were originally marketed as a way for parents and teachers to start up their own provision; in fact, very few free schools have been set up in this way and those that succeed tend to be established and sustained by highly influential parents, with strong access to professional and political networks, like Toby Young, founder of the West London Free School. The majority of free schools are now run by religious organisations, existing schools or, increasingly, by multi-academy 'chains' or trusts.

But if few parents are involved in the actual establishment and day-to-day running of the new schools, how much are these schools improving the rights of access of poorer parents (another avowed focus of the 'school choice' lobby) to high-attaining schools? Well, it probably depends on what type of poor parent is seeking access. Four years in, it seems that the freedoms given to academies and free schools to draw up their own catchment areas, set their admissions criteria and manage exclusions only increase the power of schools to choose parents, not the other way round. Like a certain category of church school before them, the new schools are keen to attract highly motivated, organised families who value education, leaving families and children with more entrenched and complex problems, be that extreme poverty or special needs, at the school gate.

Research published in August 2014 by London University's Institute of Education found that while the majority of free schools were in disadvantaged areas as intended and were recruiting more ethnic minority pupils, they had fewer children eligible for free school meals than in the local area. In primary free schools, the children entering reception classes had on average higher prior attainment levels. Chris Keates, general secretary of the National Association of Schoolmasters Union of Women Teachers, told the Independent,

> Millions of pounds of taxpayers' money is being poured into a handful of free schools. Most of those qualified for funding on the basis they were being established in deprived areas. Yet they appear to have no real desire to serve the communities and are instead using their freedom to exclude those children who need the most help.[31]

Of course, such mechanisms only add to and aggravate, albeit in more subtle ways, a long-existing problem in the English education system which is 'with [the] exception of a couple of countries, the most socially segregated in the developed world' according to the Sutton Trust.[32] A small but powerful private sector selects children on the basis of parental wealth and a range of academic tests of variable difficulty; and, as we have seen, the remaining grammar schools largely educate the more affluent. Among the country's 'top' five hundred comprehensives, Sutton Trust researchers found that socially selective schools tended to be voluntary-aided faith schools or converter academies. Both of these types of school are their own 'admission authorities' and set their own admission criteria.[33] In 2010, Barnardo's, the children's charity argued that selective school admission policies had led to almost half of Britain's poor children being siphoned into just a quarter of our schools.[34]

In such an active school market, it is not surprising that the new free schools and academies created by government are taking advantage of their admissions freedoms. As the Academies Commission (2013) reported, when market forces enter education systems this 'provides incentives for schools to avoid particular, vulnerable pupils who might be seen as detrimental to the school's attainment profile'.[35] In 2012, five of the 24 first-wave free schools had objections to their admission criteria upheld/partially upheld.[36] Two of these were censured for giving priority to pupils who had attended privately-owned, fee-paying schools.[37]

The Academies Commission also expressed concern that the academies programme in England, designed to increase competition between schools, could have a detrimental effect on the central provision of local authority services for pupils with special needs (SEN). Although academies are supposed to accept any child whose SEN Statement names the school, the academy can appeal to the Education Secretary to make a different determination. The Commission found the implications of this baffled even legal experts and feared a population of hard-to-place children could emerge and could increase pupil segregation by social and ethnic background, one of the findings in Sweden as a result of free school reforms.[38]

A fifth of English state schools are now religious, with worrying implications for community cohesion and inclusion. The Schools Adjudicator has found faith schools such as the London Oratory[39] which educates the son of the Deputy Prime Minister, and the Grey Coat Hospital School,[40] which took Michael Gove's daughter in September 2014, had faith criteria in their admissions criteria which went beyond what the Schools Admission Code 2012 allows. In March 2015, it emerged that the Grey Coat School was asking parents to enclose a cheque for £96 when confirming acceptance of a place at the school. Requesting such payments goes against the Code.[41]

Both these schools are described as 'comprehensive'; in reality their intake is heavily skewed towards the top of the ability range. Even when faith schools are compliant with the Code, the ability to give priority based on faith can lead to negative consequences, the Schools Adjudicator said in the Annual Report 2013. She noted that 'looked-after children', normally prioritised because of their 'looked-after' status, could be discriminated against if they were not of the faith.[42] The Adjudicator also heard from local authorities that some schools which were their own admission authorities (these would include all academies and free schools) were refusing to cooperate with the Fair Access Protocol.[43]

One of the findings of the global-wide OECD review on the impact of competition on schools was that schools were forced to spend more on marketing and less on actual education: similar developments can be seen in the UK. For example, the National Audit Office[44] found Durand Academy Trust had paid over £500k to Personal Lobbying & Media Relations (PLMR) for 'services'. These included the 'Shine a Light on Opportunity' campaign which resulted in '23 mentions of Durand in Parliament' and numerous references by Michael Gove when he was Secretary of State for Education.[45] Durand has since been plunged into controversy over related party transactions, transfer of land and setting up a membership-only club initially registered on school premises.[46]

Public relations firms are increasingly offering marketing packages to academies and free schools. Communitas PR, for example, will offer advice on public relations, marketing and reputation management. It was hired by Park View Education Trust to manage the fall-out from the Trojan Horse affair when all the Trust's academies were judged Inadequate.[47]

The OECD report on market mechanisms (introducing more 'choice', vouchers, etc.) in education also found that such mechanisms did not lead to greater innovation.[48] In fact, the opposite was true in many cases – schools became more traditional in outlook. The report found that UK-based researchers said competition between schools resulted in increased emphasis on school uniforms and teaching academic subjects at the expense of vocational ones. The Academies Commission agreed. It concluded innovation was stifled by league tables.[49]

Competitive systems which encourage schools to raise results have negative effects. The OECD UK Economic Survey 2011 said the excessive emphasis on exam results in England risked teaching to the test, 'gaming' and neglecting other essential skills.[50] But this emphasis has not abated. Competition between schools has grown fiercer and risks resulting in pseudo-improvement: results that look good on paper but have actually reduced the standard of education received by children. Tony Little, Eton's headmaster, echoed this concern in August 2014 when he said it was wrong 'to confuse league table success with a good education'.[51]

Effective schooling was difficult to measure, said the OECD, with researchers unclear about whether exam results were reliable indicators of school quality. Most believed value-added scores were needed and prior ability levels of pupils should be taken into account. It was not easy to separate 'good', 'average' or 'bad' schools using test scores alone. This led some researchers to conclude 'publishing league tables to inform parental school choice is a somewhat meaningless exercise'.[52] The introduction of the new 'Progress 8' accountability measure in 2014, while still not bedded in, is a recognition of the failure of the over simplistic and now moribund 5 A*–C headline figure.

For over thirty years UK politicians and policy makers have worked hard to shore up the myth that further competition, more emphasis on results, greater 'parental choice' and reduced local accountability will create better schools. To help establish the success of the model, free schools and academies have been granted greater resources and received more political, media and corporate backing from organisations which stand to gain from running schools – all in the aim of proving public systems of education a failure.

Over the past five years, in particular, we have been told that private effort, and for-profit enterprise, can solve issues that state education has been grappling with for many decades and in a society that has become progressively more, not less, unequal. We have witnessed the disdain of many so-called 'new providers' in the face both of existing state school success and the continuing impact of deep social and economic inequality on students, teachers and schools. The for-profit bandwagon is also driven by an arrogant refusal to consider proposals for improvement coming from those with long experience of working, teaching and running state education. Such ideas are dismissively written off as the ravings of 'The Blob'.[53]

Writing about free schools in the early days, writer, editor and former teacher Laura McInerney identified some of the problems that have come in the wake of the new schools market.

When setting up a new school many think the problems of 'old schools' won't follow them. They will, and on top of that you will need to maintain a 'perfect veneer' to prove your place in the local marketplace because you will have created a competitive market . . . new school leaders ignore the fact that local schools strug-gle to get Headteachers, or afford new buildings, and believe that these resources will 'somehow' appear at their new school. But of course, it is not that simple . . . Remember, if another school nearby isn't already doing what you wish to deliver, there's probably a good reason . . . New schools soon become not so new and many start to face some of the very human problems – of time, money, staff illness and burnout – that face some of the 'old' schools'. [54]

Such arguments were prescient as was the suggestion that school leaders would do better to collaborate rather than compete; although free schools and academies have been handed, as we explore above, some useful tools in terms of improving their position in the local schools market. Add to this the high political stakes and sheer human pride attached to the perceived success of the competitive model, and the massive amount of money potentially to be made in making education an explicitly for-profit business. Despite the manifest weaknesses of the choice and competition agenda, the Coalition government had simply invested too much political, and financial, capital in the idea to shift its thinking in the face of the evidence.

Educational guru John Hattie puts the core myth-busting argument with clarity and force, 'We are so obsessed with free schools and academies, but what a distraction. Isn't it a con? You give parents this belief about choice. They can choose the school. But they can't choose the teacher.' It is, he added, 'teachers . . . rather than school structures of systems [that] improve learning'.[55] We turn to this all-important issue in Chapter 6.

Notes

1 Jenny Turner, 'Barely Under Control', *London Review Of Books*, 7 May 2015.
2 http://www.theguardian.com/education/2014/oct/28/slowdown-schools-converting-academies accessed 28 January 2015.
3 https://www.gov.uk/government/news/elizabeth-truss-responds-to-nao-free-school-report accessed 28 January 2015.
4 http://www.lkmco.org/article/press-release-six-predictable-failures-free-schools-27032011 accessed 28 January 2015.
5 https://www.gov.uk/government/news/prime-minister-more-new-free-schools-than-ever-before-to-raise-standards-and-increase-choice accessed 28 January 2015.
6 http://www.theguardian.com/commentisfree/2013/jul/31/free-schools-success-ed-miliband-admit accessed 17 August 2015.
7 http://www.bbc.co.uk/news/uk-england-beds-bucks-herts-26233131 accessed 28 January 2015.
8 https://www.gov.uk/government/uploads/system/uploads/attachment_data/file/256056/131107_Letter_to_Baroness_Jones_of_Whithurch.pdf accessed 28 January 2015.
9 https://www.whatdotheyknow.com/request/names_of_new_local_authority_sch#incoming-456854 accessed 28 January 2015.
10 http://www.localschoolsnetwork.org.uk/2015/03/free-schools-policy-exchange-finds-no-positive-effect-for-schools-nearby/ accessed 28 January 2015.
11 http://www.telegraph.co.uk/education/8734830/Free-schools-Bradfords-Kings-Academy-leads-the-way.html accessed 28 January 2015.
12 http://www.thetelegraphandargus.co.uk/news/local/localbrad/11389080.Kings_Science_Academy_principal_dismissed/ accessed 28 January 2015.

13 http://www.yorkshirepost.co.uk/news/main-topics/education/two-more-former-members-of-staff-at-bradford-s-kings-science-academy-charged-over-fraud-claims-1-7153414 accessed 28 January 2015.

14 http://www.asa.org.uk/Rulings/Adjudications.aspx?SearchTerms=E-Act#2 accessed 28 January 2015.

15 http://webarchive.nationalarchives.gov.uk/20141124154759/http://www.ofsted.gov.uk/resources/e-act-multi-academy-trust-inspection-outcome-letter accessed 28 January 2015.

16 http://www.localschoolsnetwork.org.uk/2014/12/23-academies-changed-hands-in-13-months-but-the-dfe-wont-say-how-much-this-cost-the-taxpayer/ accessed 28 January 2015.

17 http://www.theguardian.com/education/2014/apr/06/michael-gove-failing-free-schools accessed 28 January 2015.

18 http://www.publications.parliament.uk/pa/cm201415/cmselect/cmeduc/258/258.pdf accessed 28 January 2015.

19 http://www.localschoolsnetwork.org.uk/2013/12/mixed-reaction-to-nao-report-into-free-schools/ accessed 28 January 2015.

20 http://www.publications.parliament.uk/pa/cm201314/cmselect/cmpubacc/941/94104.htm accessed 28 January 2015.

21 http://www.publications.parliament.uk/pa/cm201314/cmselect/cmpubacc/941/94104.htm accessed 28 January 2015.

22 https://news.tes.co.uk/b/news/2014/08/06/free-schools-open-in-poor-areas-but-intakes-better-off.aspx accessed 28 January 2015.

23 Department for Education School Performance Tables 2014 accessed 28 January 2015.

24 http://www.theguardian.com/politics/2014/may/10/gove-lunatic-raid-free-schools accessed 28 January 2015.

25 http://www.theguardian.com/politics/2014/may/10/gove-lunatic-raid-free-schools accessed 17 August 2015.

26 http://www.publications.parliament.uk/pa/cm201314/cmselect/cmpubacc/941/94104.htm accessed 28 January 2015.

27 http://www.nao.org.uk/wp-content/uploads/2013/12/10314-001-Free-Schools-Book-Copy.pdf accessed 28 January 2015.

28 http://www.everythingfreeschools.co.uk/2014/05/07/spending-on-free-schools/ Website no longer available accessed 28 January 2015.

29 http://www.independent.co.uk/news/education/education-news/exclusive-anger-over-new-free-school-that-may-be-be-britains-mostexpensive-9222364.html accessed 28 January 2015.

30 http://www.independent.co.uk/news/education/education-news/exclusive-anger-over-new-free-school-that-may-be-be-britains-mostexpensive-9222364.html accessed 28 January 2015.

31 http://www.independent.co.uk/news/education/education-news/governments-flagship-free-schools-accused-of-allowing-stealth-selection-as-they-fail-to-admit-poorest-kids-9652592.html accessed 28 January 2015.

Choice will improve education in England

32 http://www.suttontrust.com/wp-content/uploads/2013/02/
CONFUSION-IN-THE-RANKS-SMITHERS-LEAGUE-TABLES-
FINAL.pdf accessed 28 January 2015.

33 The Sutton Trust looked at the top 500 comprehensive state
schools when measured by five good GCSEs including English
and Maths and at the top 500 measured according to success in
the relatively new English Baccalaureate (EBacc) league table
measure. http://www.suttontrust.com/researcharchive/selective-
comprehensives/ accessed 28 January 2015.

34 Barnardord *Unlocking the Gates* 2010 http://www.lgcplus.com/
Journals/3/Files/2010/8/27/unlocking_the_gates.pdf accessed 28
January 2015.

35 https://www.thersa.org/globalassets/pdfs/reports/unleashing-great-
ness.pdf accessed 28 January 2015.

36 Decisions searchable at https://www.gov.uk/government/publica
tions?keywords=&publication_filter_option=decisions&topics[]=a
ll&departments[]=office-of-the-schools-adjudicator&official_docu-
ment_status=all&world_locations[]=all&from_date=&to_date=
accessed 28 January 2015.

37 As above.

38 https://www.thersa.org/globalassets/pdfs/reports/unleashing-
greatness.pdf accessed 28 January 2015.

39 Decisions searchable at https://www.gov.uk/government/publica
tions?keywords=&publication_filter_option=decisions&topics[]=a
ll&departments[]=office-of-the-schools-adjudicator&official_docu-
ment_status=all&world_locations[]=all&from_date=&to_date=
accessed 28 January 2015.

40 As above.

41 http://schoolsweek.co.uk/exclusive-gove-and-pm-school-made-
forbidden-donation-request/ accessed 28 January 2015.

42 Office of the Schools Adjudicator annual report September 2012
to August 2013 http://media.education.gov.uk/assets/files/pdf/o/
osa%20annual%20report%201213%20final%20word%20version.
pdf (p. 32) accessed 28 January 2015.

43 Op. cit., p. 35.

44 http://www.nao.org.uk/wp-content/uploads/2014/11/Investigation-
into-the-Education-Funding-Agencys-oversight-of-related-party-
transactions-at-Durand-Academy.pdf accessed 28 January 2015.

45 http://www.welovead.com/en/works/details/780CjnqD accessed
28 January 2015.

46 http://data.parliament.uk/writtenevidence/committeeevidence.
svc/evidencedocument/public-accounts-committee/education-funding-
agency-and-department-for-education-financial-statements-recall/
oral/17774.html accessed 28 January 2015.

Choice will improve education in England

47 http://www.communitas-pr.co.uk/index.php?page=what-we-offer accessed 28 January 2015.
48 http://www.oecd.org/officialdocuments/publicdisplaydocumentp df/?cote=EDU/WKP%282010%2915&docLanguage=En accessed 28 January 2015.
49 https://www.thersa.org/globalassets/pdfs/reports/unleashing-greatness.pdf accessed 28 January 2015.
50 http://www.localschoolsnetwork.org.uk/2011/06/too-much-emphasis-on-grades-is-cause-of-concern-say-oecd/ accessed 28 January 2015.
51 http://www.telegraph.co.uk/education/educationnews/11010748/ Eton-headmaster-warns-Government-Dont-put-British-children-in-a-Chinese-straitjacket.html accessed 28 January 2015.
52 http://www.oecd.org/officialdocuments/publicdisplaydocumentp df/?cote=EDU/WKP%282010%2915&docLanguage=En accessed 28 January 2015.
53 http://www.dailymail.co.uk/debate/article-2298146/I-refuse-surrender-Marxist-teachers-hell-bent-destroying-schools-Education-Secretary-berates-new-enemies-promise-opposing-plans.html and http:// civitas.org.uk/education/POTB.php accessed 28 January 2015.
54 McInerney, Laura, op. cit.
55 'Panel-beaters don't have to learn Shakespeare', *Times Educational Supplement*, 1 May 2015.

Academies raise standards

This myth is a direct offshoot of the myth about the merits of competition in a schools market. But it has also acquired its own distinct and separate sheen. Over the past decade and a half, these three simple words, 'academies raise standards', have taken on the force of a quasi-Biblical truth in public life. According to one of the key architects of New Labour's academies programme, Andrew Adonis, 'academies are all about 'giving children an equal start in life'.[1] Unrealistically positive, and sometimes worryingly partial, interpretations of the data abound in pro-academy literature, constantly reaffirmed by government sources, such as this typical statement from the Department for Education in late 2013: 'The sponsored academies programme has been a huge success in transforming the fortunes of the weakest, most challenging schools.'[2] Anyone who interprets the evidence in a more sober light is judged to be blind to the obvious, resistant to school improvement or deliberately troublesome – or all three.

The question at issue here is not: do we need high-performing all-ability schools ensuring a high quality of teaching and learning, constant enrichment of the curriculum and the maintenance of good discipline? The answer to all those questions is clearly 'yes'. The question at issue is, in fact, much simpler: does the evidence show that academisation has proved itself to be the sole route to this kind of high quality schooling? Is this the best method? Have other kinds of state schools, such as those within the much-traduced maintained sector, managed to improve at the same or indeed even at a better rate? Could it be that the route to improvement lies, as Andrew Adonis himself argued, in changes in 'leadership, ethos, discipline . . . and the quality of teaching and learning' rather than in semi-private governance?[3] And finally, has academisation, like some of the other independent state school models that we looked at in the last chapter, come at a price?

So let's leave the quasi-religious tone behind and look at the simple facts.

Sponsored academies were first set up by Labour in 2002 as a way of turning round persistently underperforming schools in disadvantaged areas. Sponsors were encouraged to support the school both financially and by taking control of governance.

Even in these early days, the Department for Children, Schools and Families (DfCSF) talked up academy success. But the Commons Education Committee was not convinced. In 2005, it accused the DfCSF of promoting a scheme which had not been properly evaluated and recommended the £5bn funding for academies should be withheld until academies were shown to be cost effective. The Committee said:

> We recognise that secondary education has failed in some inner city areas and we understand the temptation to believe that Academies are the solution. Yet £5 billion is a lot of money to commit to one programme . . . Whilst we welcome the government's desire to invest resources in areas of educational underachievement, we consider that the rapid expansion of the Academy policy comes at the expense of rigorous evaluation.[4]

Academies raise standards

The first assessment of academies by PriceWaterhouse-Coopers (PwC) in the same year also presented a mixed picture of their success. The government did not publish this report on the grounds there were too few academies. However, Freedom of Information requests by the media forced its publication. The Education Network (TEN) accused ministers of 'misleading' the public by promoting an image of success that was at odds with the facts.[5]

In 2007, the Public Accounts Committee said 'Academic results have improved faster in academies than in other schools'.[6] But it made the mistake of comparing previously-underperforming schools with all other schools. Calculating the rate of improvement from a lower base is bound to result in a larger improvement rate.

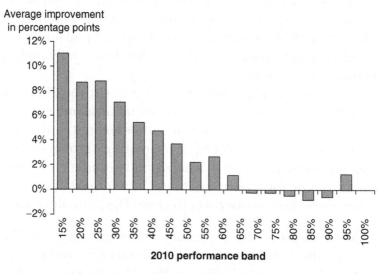

Figure 5.1 Change in performance in 2011 among maintained schools by 2010 results

Page 8 House of Commons Briefing Paper *Sponsored Academies: Statistics Standard Note*: SN/SG/4719. Last updated: 28 February 2012 (downloadable here http://researchbriefings.parliament.uk/ResearchBriefing/Summary/SN04719 #fullreport) accessed 24 August 2015.

This was made clear when the House of Commons analysed growth in the GCSE benchmark, and compared exam results to the previous year's performance. Those schools with a GCSE benchmark (five A*-Cs including English and maths) previously below 35 per cent grew on average by over 6 per cent. Those previously between 35 per cent and 65 per cent grew between 1 per cent and 5 per cent. And those previously above 65 per cent saw their results, again on average, fall.

Any group of schools which are largely on the left-hand side of the graph will tend to increase their results at a faster rate than schools overall. To evaluate whether being an academy increases results it is necessary to compare them to schools with similar prior GCSE results. (Although the House of Commons analysis was only concerned with the change from 2010 to 2011, the same correlation has been clear each year. Statisticians would describe this trend as 'reversion to the mean'.)

The Public Accounts Committee, however, made another important point when it concluded academies could be 'an expensive way of tackling underperformance' and the government needed to balance this expenditure and any benefits it might bring with other programmes intended to raise performance.[7]

A year later, the Sutton Trust warned:

Academics are in danger of being regarded by politicians as a panacea for a broad range of education problems. Given the variable performance of Academies to date, conversion to an Academy may not always be the best route to improvement. Care needs to be taken to ensure that Academies are the 'best fit' solution to the problem at hand.[8]

Also in 2008, PwC concluded there was 'insufficient evidence to make a definitive judgement about academies as a model for school improvement'. It discovered academies which had improved used similar methods found in improving local authority schools:

> In their efforts to improve teaching and learning, Academies are generally operating in similar ways to improving schools in the [local authority] maintained sector, namely monitoring and improving the quality of lessons, ensuring appropriate continuing professional development, and tracking and monitoring pupil progress.[9]

In 2009, a University of Birmingham report looked at academies established between 2002 and 2007. It found 'no clear evidence' that academies produced better results than local authority schools with equivalent intakes. The author had 'considerable sympathy with the aims of the [Academy] programme' but wrote 'it is not immediately clear that they are doing a better job overall than their colleagues in non-Academy schools in similar circumstances, for whom I have similar admiration'.[10]

Despite these repeated warnings that academy conversion was no panacea and that the evidence showed that non-academies in similar circumstances were doing equally as well, in the summer of 2010 the coalition government pushed through the Academies Bill with the speed usually reserved for national emergencies. This allowed schools judged 'Good' or 'Outstanding' to become academies, and increased their funding by providing them with a 'top slice' of local authority funding that had previously been held back for collective use.

The ink was still wet on this Bill when the National Audit Office (NAO) published its findings into the academies programme. It noted that some sponsored academies had performed 'exceptionally well' but others had made 'little progress'. It warned:

'It cannot be assumed, however, that academies' performance to date is an accurate predictor of how the model will perform when generalised more widely.'[11]

Nevertheless, the coalition pressed ahead and was encouraged by a report into academies set up by the Labour government by the London School of Economics (LSE).[12] This painted a 'relatively positive' picture of Labour academies and said results in neighbouring schools had also risen. But these higher results coincided with a national rise in exam results and, the LSE noted, with a rise in the quality of intake in the academies. Significantly the LSE warned that their findings could not be used to justify conversion of previously good or outstanding schools nor changing primary schools into academies.[13] That did not stop the coalition repeatedly using its findings to justify perhaps the most contentious aspect of the Gove revolution: enforced academisation.

Schools Minister, Nick Gibb, told the House of Commons in January 2012 that academies raised results:

> There is also strong evidence (including from London School of Economics, 2011, Public Accounts Committee, 2011, National Audit Office, 2010, and PwC, 2008) of the benefits, in terms of raised standards, of secondary schools becoming academies. There is no reason why this intervention should not work as well if not better in primary schools as it does in secondary schools.[14]

But, as we've seen, the NAO and PwC did not wholeheartedly endorse academies and the LSE report had warned against using their findings to justify mass conversion.

Stephen Machin, one of the authors of the LSE report, became so concerned that the findings were being used to justify the coalition's academy conversion programme that he told *The Guardian* in April 2012:

It may be, in due course, that these new academies do deliver performance improvements. But we know nothing of this yet, and translating the evidence from the old programme over to the new, without appropriate reservations about whether the findings can be generalised, is, at the moment, a step too far.[15]

The coalition, however, continued to say that 'sponsored academies' improvement in GCSEs outstripped other schools: 'The secondary school performance tables show that standards are rising in sponsored academies at a record rate – and more than 5 times as quickly than in all state-funded schools.'[16]

The coalition, whether by ignorance or design, was still comparing the rate of improvement in sponsored academies with all other schools. But sponsored academies were mainly schools which had previously underperformed while all schools included those with already strong results. The government can't say it has not been warned about making such a basic statistical error. Channel 4 had fact-checked a speech made by the then Secretary of State for Education, Michael Gove, on 4 January 2012, when he announced: '[In] the 166 sponsored academies with results in both 2010 and 2011, the percentage point increase in pupils achieving five plus A*–C including English and maths was double that of maintained schools.'[17]

FactCheck reminded Gove that these sponsored academies were established from previously underperforming schools and 'If you compare the exam results of an underperforming school to an average one, you are starting from a lower base, and it may be that the worse things are to begin with, the quicker they improve'.[18]

Channel 4 was not the only fact-checker. Henry Stewart of The Local Schools Network also crunched the numbers.

In 2012 the proportion of pupils who gained the benchmark five plus GCSEs A*–C (or equivalent) including maths and English in sponsored academies rose by 3.1 per cent compared with 0.6 per cent in all non-academies. But remember, all non-academies included previously high-performing schools. It would be expected, therefore, that the rate of improvement would be higher in the sponsored academies because, as noted above, it is calculated from a lower base.

What Henry Stewart's research for the Local Schools Network found was that if sponsored academies are compared with similar non-academies, the increase was remarkably similar. Henry compared the results of schools whose GCSE benchmark score was in the 20–40 per cent range in 2011. He found academies increased their score by 7.8 per cent and non-academies by 7.7 per cent. It made little difference whether the school was an academy or not.

The same was true when Henry studied a longer time frame between 2008 and 2011. Henry looked at the growth in schools where less than 35 per cent reached the benchmark in 2008: 46 academies and 594 non-academies. Academies under 35 per cent in 2008 saw average growth in results of 18.6 per cent from 2008 to 2011. That is impressive and well done to those schools on a remarkable increase. However, the non-academies that were under 35 per cent in 2008 saw growth of 19.1 per cent in results from 2008 to 2011. So the non-academies, almost 600 of them, saw an average increase that was slightly greater than that of the academies.[19]

This is before taking account of GCSE equivalent exams like BTECs. These are vocational examinations which were judged as the equivalent of up to four GCSEs. Much use of equivalents was regarded by the DfE as gaming the system and, following the Wolf reforms in 2014, are mainly no longer included in the GCSE benchmark. Results in sponsored academies fell from 43 per cent to 29 per cent when equivalent exams were removed. Results in non-academies also fell but not as far: they dropped from 45 per cent to 34 per cent without equivalents.

The *Daily Telegraph* noticed in early 2012 that 'Academy schools "inflate results with easy qualifications"'.[20] But this 'gaming' the system had been noted by PwC in 2008: it had found some academies had used vocational courses to boost improvement more quickly.

Michael Gove has faced two ways on this issue of equivalents. On the one hand, he has criticised such practices. On the other hand, he has lavishly praised the results of schools that have used equivalent exams. A paper deposited in the House of Commons Library on 19 April 2012[21] showed results at four academies in the much-lauded Harris chain dropped considerably when equivalent exams were excluded:

Harris Academy Peckham – 50 per cent to 30 per cent

Harris Academy South Norwood – 75 per cent to 46 per cent

Harris Academy Purley – 61 per cent to 45 per cent

Harris Academy Falconwood – 57 per cent to 47 per cent

Removing equivalent exams from some sponsored academies' results in 2011 all but wiped out the proportion of pupils that reached the benchmark:

The Steiner Academy Hereford – 70 per cent to 0 per cent

The Isle of Sheppey Academy – 35 per cent to 4 per cent

Skegness Academy – 45 per cent to 1 per cent

By 2013, Harris academies used fewer equivalent examinations. But other chains, such as Ormiston and Priory Federation, used slightly more while Oasis, Grace and E-Act increased their use of equivalent exams significantly

between 2011 and 2013. Concern was so great about performance at some academy chains by March 2014 that the
DfE 'paused' 14 from taking on more academies.[22] Grace
and E-Act were two of them.

Henry Stewart found the average proportion of pupils
in 2013 reaching the benchmark when equivalent exams
were removed fell more in some academy chains than in
local authorities. Out of 151 local authorities, only two had
an average GCSE benchmark below 35 per cent in 2013,
once equivalents are removed. However, of the top seven
academy chains (based on number of sponsored academies that were more than five years) four had an average
figure below 35 per cent – even only taking account of
schools which had been academies for at least five years.[23]

But heavy use of equivalent exams is not confined to
academy chains or sponsored academies. At Perry Beeches
The Academy, a converter academy much-praised by
Michael Gove for achieving well above the national average, the proportion reaching the benchmark in 2013 fell
from 80 per cent (well above the national average of 60.6
per cent for state secondary schools) to 53 per cent (the
national average) when equivalent exams were removed.

Michael Gove was keen to see a return to 'traditional'
subjects like history, geography or languages and liked
to give the impression that academies were making these
more widely available in disadvantaged areas. In fact the
reverse has been the case.

As the graph below shows, students are less likely to
achieve a history or geography GCSE if they attend a
sponsored academy. This is true when you compare all
academies to all non-academies, but also when you compare those with previously low results or only those for
schools where more than 40 per cent are rated as disadvantaged using the DFE's measure.

The same is true of languages or for the English Baccalaureate (EBacc). When similar schools are compared,

Academies raise standards

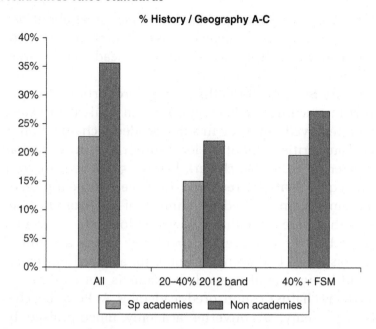

% History / Geography A-C

Figure 5.2 Academies/Non-Academies % Geography A–C

students are far less likely to take or achieve the EBacc in a sponsored academy. Students are less likely to take a language GCSE if they are in a sponsored academy – both overall and when compared to similar schools.[24]

The government has curtailed the use of equivalent exams by reducing the number that will count towards league tables from 2014. This is likely to affect sponsored and some converter academies to a greater extent than non-academies.

The Academies Commission (2013) agreed with Henry's research: results in sponsored academies in 2011 were slightly lower than in similar non-academy schools when equivalent (non-GCSE) exams were removed from the figures. Many previously underperforming non-academy schools in disadvantaged areas had done just as well as similar academies, the Academies Commission reported.[25] The only sponsored academies that improved more than similar non-academies were those which had already benefited from the City Challenge, the Commission found.

A DfE report buried in the DfE website and not widely publicised, showed the City Challenge had been more successful in raising performance than the sponsored academies programme.[26] Yet the government ignored its own research and continued to push the line that sponsored academies are improving more rapidly than all other schools.

Converter academies, too, are raising results, the government says. Michael Gove told the Education Select Committee on 31 January 2012 that converter academies are helping to drive up standards, particularly for the disadvantaged.[27]

But the evidence supporting this statement did not exist. A Freedom of Information request[28] first yielded a reply which showed the DfE did not know the difference between sponsored and converter academies. When challenged, it provided evidence from Sweden and the United States but nothing about English converter academies.

Henry Stewart's analysis found pupils who attract the pupil premium do better in non-academies. This confirmed earlier analysis into sponsored academies set up by Labour by Stephen Machin, one of the authors of the misused LSE report. In 2013 he co-authored a paper with Olmo Silva which looked at the performance of children at the lower end of the ability distribution, the so-called 'tail', in these academies.[29] They tentatively concluded:

> Whilst there is a paucity of robust and coherent evidence to draw upon, it does not seem unreasonable to say that, on balance, the evidence that does exist at best shows only small beneficial effects on overall pupil performance and very little consistent evidence of improvements for tail students.[30]

Academies raise standards

All the data above has been based on the performance of secondary schools – there were no primary academies before the coalition came to power in 2010. But Henry Stewart's analysis of the 2013 Key Stage 2 SAT results showed the biggest increases in performance were in non-academies.[31] 95 per cent of the most improved primary schools in terms of SAT results were non-academies.[32]

As the primary academy programme is new, results are only available over one or two years. However, the first analysis of primary academies with non-academies shows a dramatic difference. For instance, when schools below the 60 per cent floor target in 2012 are compared, we find that the increase in results in non-academies was over twice that of academies:

Sponsored academies: + 5.1 per cent

Non-academies: + 13.2 per cent

Henry Stewart's analysis has never been challenged by the DfE. Indeed the two interpretations were compared at the High Court in June 2014, when the DfE was challenged on its right to force The Warren School to become an academy.

Faced with the need to justify its claims in court, the DfE argued only that 'results in sponsored academies were marginally higher than in a group of similar local authority schools' (quote from High Court judgement).

However, even this marginally higher figure was based on figures that included GCSE equivalents. The DfE's own document 'Attainment at Key Stage 4 by pupils in Academies 2011' found the marginally higher figure for sponsored academies (46 per cent v. 45.7 per cent for similar non-academies) fell to 32.6 per cent for academies v. 35.6 per cent for similar non-academies once equivalents were stripped out.[33] The earlier analysis and the Warren court case indicated that, once equivalents are stripped out, any impression of better performance by academies would disappear. This was confirmed when the DfE released school-by-school GCSE results, based on the new Wolf benchmark that will be used in 2014.

Range, WOLF 2012	Increase in GCSE benchmark 2012–13	
	Sponsored academies	Non-academies
0.0 per cent	12.4 per cent	16.3 per cent
20.0 per cent	5.9 per cent	6.2 per cent
40.0 per cent	1.1 per cent	2.2 per cent
60.0 per cent	–1.0 per cent	–0.2 per cent
80.0 per cent	–7.3 per cent	–1.5 per cent

Figure 5.3 Growth in GCSE benchmark results, comparing schools starting from similar GCSE figures in 2012

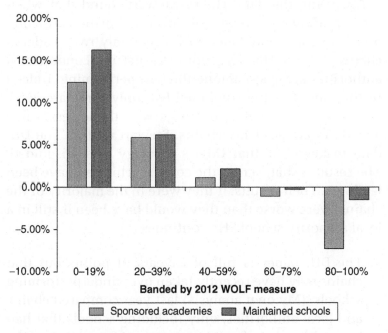

Figure 5.4 Wolf GCSE: Change 2012 to 2013

Academies raise standards

If we split schools into 20 per cent bands according to their 2012 GCSE results, we can compare the growth of similar schools. In every one of these bands, the GCSE results of the non-academies grew at a faster rate than those of the sponsored academies.

A new, if closely related, problem has emerged more recently, with a report from the Department of Education pinpointing the serious underperformance of many of the academy chains. Of the 20 academy chains (being those multi-academy trusts with at least 5 schools), only three have a 'value added' score that is above the national average. This confirms why those who talk so frequently about 'high-performing academy chains' refer only to ARK and Harris. These emerge strongly from the DfE tables (along with the Diocese of Westminster). But they are the exception. Fully 85 per cent of academy chains are underperforming.

Analysing the data, Henry Stewart found that when the top academy chains and local authorities are combined, (using value added measures) only two academy chains (Ark and Harris) get onto the list, but London local authorities are again among the best performing. Indeed in the top 50 of the combined list, only three are academy chains. Meanwhile in the 50 with the lowest 'value added', 15 are academy chains. Stewart writes, 'The DfE data makes clear that Gove's ideology was misguided. The result is that, across the country, children have been let down. Their results, if they were in the majority of the chains, were worse than they would have been if still in a local authority school.' He continues,

> The DfE paper is full of caveats. It points out that chains may have recently taken over underperforming schools. (My own analysis) last year compared chains and local authorities, only including schools that had been with a chain for at least 5 years. I found that, of the

7 largest chains, 5 had an average GCSE score (without equivalents) of 35% or less. Of 152 local authorities, only 2 had an average of 35% or less. (Also, the DfE calculation adjusts for the length of time a school has been in a chain.) The figures for LAs only include schools in their area that are not academies. The paper also notes that LA figures may be lower than otherwise because so many of their Good and Outstanding schools have become academies. Given this fact it is truly remarkable that the local authority 'value-added' figure is so strong.[34]

Academy chains are principally the creation of the Coalition government. It initially protected them from Ofsted inspection and did not require them to reveal how the funding they receive is spent at a school level. Even now, Ofsted can inspect them but cannot deliver a judgement on the chain as a whole. The Labour Party has begun to question this hands-off approach. In early 2015, Education spokesman Tristram Hunt argued that while 'chains can be an incredibly important architecture in a school innovation system . . . I see too many schools struggling with second-rate academy chains, and I want to set them free'.[35] Henry Stewart concludes that Hunt's

> suggestion that schools should be allowed to escape from poorly performing chains is a step in the right direction. However he surely needs to be tougher in exposing the scandal of the academy chains. They are a massive experiment with our children's future, based on ideology rather than evidence, and it is now clear that the experiment has failed.[36]

When the coalition came to power there were two major educational programmes for which evidence existed of their impact. The first is the 'London Challenge', widely

Academies raise standards

recognised as having transformed education in the capital, taking the performance of London schools from below the national average to well above it. The new government chose not to learn lessons from this.

In contrast, the research on the academies programme showed, as we have described in detail above, decidedly mixed results. The coalition chose to focus its resources on these. The DfE's Permanent Secretary described this as the government's principle means of school improvement. The Conservative government, elected with a slim majority in May 2015, is clearly pledged to create and support more academies, despite the clear lack of evidence of their success. For all the investment and all the loudly claimed benefits of academy status the evidence – once they are compared to similar schools and without equivalents – shows that improvements in academies are less than in maintained schools.

Notes

1 http://www.independent.co.uk/news/education/schools/andrew-adonis-on-academies-its-about-giving-children-an-equal-start-in-life-2369616.html accessed 28 January 2015.
2 https://www.gov.uk/government/news/intervention-in-academies accessed 11 November 2013.
3 Andrew Adonis, *Education, Education, Education*, Biteback, 2012, p. 19.
4 http://www.publications.parliament.uk/pa/cm200405/cmselect/cmeduski/86/86.pdf accessed 26 June 2014.
5 http://news.bbc.co.uk/1/hi/education/4638687.stm accessed 26 June 2014.
6 http://www.publications.parliament.uk/pa/cm200607/cmselect/cmpubacc/402/402.pdf (p. 4), accessed 17 August 2015.
7 http://www.publications.parliament.uk/pa/cm200607/cmselect/cmpubacc/402/402.pdf accessed 28 January 2015.
8 http://www.suttontrust.com/wp-content/uploads/2008/12/AcademiesReportFinal2.pdf accessed 28 January 2015.
9 PwC, *Academies Evaluation Fifth Annual Report*, 2008.
10 http://eprints.bham.ac.uk/598/1/Academies_paper4,_JEP.pdf accessed 28 January 2015.

Academies raise standards

11 http://www.nao.org.uk/wp-content/uploads/2010/09/1011288.pdf accessed 28 January 2015.
12 http://cee.lse.ac.uk/ceedps/ceedp123.pdf accessed 28 January 2015.
13 http://cee.lse.ac.uk/ceedps/ceedp123.pdf accessed 28 January 2015.
14 http://www.publications.parliament.uk/pa/cm201212/cmhansrd/cm120131/text/120131w0004.htm accessed 28 January 2015.
15 http://www.theguardian.com/education/2012/apr/09/labour-academies-research-coalition-programme accessed 28 January 2015.
16 https://www.gov.uk/government/news/sponsored-academies-improvement-in-gcses-outstripping-other-schools accessed 28 January 2015.
17 https://www.gov.uk/government/speeches/michael-gove-speech-on-academies accessed 28 January 2015.
18 http://blogs.channel4.com/factcheck/factcheck/8994 accessed 17 August 2015.
19 Henry Stewart 2012: www.localschoolsnetwork.org.uk/2012/02/established-academies-still-no-evidence-of-betterperformance/ accessed 28 January 2015.
20 http://www.telegraph.co.uk/education/educationnews/9059532/Academy-schools-inflate-results-with-easy-qualifications.html accessed 28 January 2015.
21 Downloadable from http://www.parliament.uk/business/publications/business-papers/commons/deposited-papers/?fd=2012-04-19&td=2012-04-19&house=1&search_term=Department+for+Education&itemId=118997 accessed 26 June 2014.
22 http://www.publications.parliament.uk/pa/cm201314/cmhansrd/cm140318/text/140318w0002.htm#140318w0002.htm_spnew53 accessed 26 June 2014.
23 Henry Stewart 2014: www.localschoolsnetwork.org.uk/2014/01/academy-chains-seriously-under-performing/ accessed 27 June 2014.
24 Henry Stewart 2014: www.localschoolsnetwork.org.uk/2014/02/pupils-in-sponsored-academies-are-less-likely-toachieve-traditional-gcses/ accessed 28 January 2015.
25 http://www.thersa.org/__data/assets/pdf_file/0020/1008038/Unleashing-greatness.pdf accessed 26 June 2014.
26 https://www.gov.uk/government/uploads/system/uploads/attachment_data/file/184093/DFE-RR215.pdf accessed 26 June 2014.
27 http://www.publications.parliament.uk/pa/cm201012/cmselect/cmeduc/uc1786-i/uc178601.htm accessed 26 June 2014.
28 https://www.whatdotheyknow.com/request/statement_by_mr_gove_re_academy accessed 26 June 2014.
29 http://cep.lse.ac.uk/pubs/download/special/cepsp29.pdf accessed 26 June 2014.

Academies raise standards

30 http://cep.lse.ac.uk/pubs/download/special/cepsp29.pdf (p. 11), accessed 17 August 2015.
31 http://www.localschoolsnetwork.org.uk/2013/12/biggest-sats-increases-are-in-non-academies/ accessed 27 June 2014.
32 http://www.localschoolsnetwork.org.uk/2014/05/lets-celebrate-all-fast-improving-primary-schools-2/ accessed 27 June 2014.
33 http://www.bailii.org/ew/cases/EWHC/Admin/2014/2252.html accessed 28 January 2015.
34 http://www.localschoolsnetwork.org.uk/2015/03/dfe-reveals-dismal-performance-of-academy-chains/ accessed 28 January 2015.
35 http://schoolsweek.co.uk/tristram-hunt-ascl-speech-full-text/ accessed 28 January 2015.
36 http://www.localschoolsnetwork.org.uk/2015/03/dfe-reveals-dismal-performance-of-academy-chains/ accessed 28 January 2015.

Teachers don't need qualifications

According to the influential 2007 McKinsey report 'How the World's Best-Performing School Systems Come Out on Top', 'The quality of an education system cannot exceed the quality of its teachers'.[1] Across the globe, it is now accepted that first-rate teaching is one of the most important elements in creating and sustaining outstanding schools. Writing about the multiple elements that go towards making Finland's education system one of the top performing in the world, Pasi Sahlberg argues that 'research and experience suggest that one factor trumps all others: the daily contributions of excellent teachers'.[2]

Until relatively recently, it would have been accepted among the chief educational and political figures in the UK that a significant period of teacher training or teacher education was both a necessary and a positive element in the building of an excellent teaching force. Not any longer. Since 2010, coalition leaders, backed by a few leading educationalists largely in the private sector, have argued that an extended pre-training period for teachers is not only unnecessary but that there are distinct advantages to some individuals having no professional qualifications at all.

Teachers don't need qualifications

Welcome then to the newest and most surprising myth among our number, an idea that would have been laughed – or booed – out of most staff rooms only five years ago: teacher qualifications, or any kind of extended teacher education, are irrelevant to the art of good teaching. Not surprisingly then, this aspect of government policy is reconfiguring our school system in profound, worrying ways. The number of unqualified teachers is on the rise. According to figures on the School Workforce in England, there are now 7,000 unqualified full-time equivalent teachers in academies and free schools.[3] Stories about the prevalence of unqualified teachers are increasingly coming to public attention. In late 2013 South Leeds academy advertised for two 'unqualified' maths teachers with a minimum of just four GCSEs. In other words, it was possible that the successful applicants could well have significantly fewer qualifications than their prospective pupils would hope to attain before leaving school.[4] A majority of those questioned in a spring 2013 NASUWT poll of 2,300 teachers said that it was becoming common practice that 'unqualified colleagues took lessons, prepared pupils for exams and assessed students' progress'.[5]

But what evidence is there that non-qualified individuals make better teachers? Is teaching really akin to the art of parenting about which, after all, we have plenty of evidence of bad as well as good intuitive practice? Is it simply a question of excellent subject knowledge, or personal dynamism, of 'picking it up as you go along'? Would we be happy to be flown by a merely 'dynamic' pilot or a surgeon who simply trusted her instincts when it came to performing an operation or do we indeed rely on properly trained professionals who are doing their work after a long period of study and observation, under the supervision of other professionals in their field? How effective can any individual be, whatever their intelligence and mastery of a particular subject, without wider knowledge about other aspects of teaching from classroom management to child development, from the history of our education system to different styles of learning?

The move to reduce teacher qualifications began soon after the election of the coalition in May 2010. In December of that same year Michael Gove announced that the heads of free schools would be able to employ people without qualified teacher status (QTS). He told the House of Commons that 'Innovation, diversity and flexibility are at the heart of the free schools policy. We want the dynamism that characterises the best independent schools to help drive up standards in the state sector.'[6] (Teachers in the private sector do not need formal qualifications.) Nick Gibb in his first tenure as Schools Minister caused further public controversy when it was reported that he told officials at the Department of Education the day after his appointment that 'I would rather have a physics graduate from Oxbridge without a PGCE teaching in a school than a physics graduate from one of the rubbish universities with a PGCE'.[7] The more emollient Anthony Seldon, Master of Wellington College, backed up the government's argument by arguing that being a teacher 'is not like becoming a doctor or vet . . . The teacher's role is much more akin to that of parent . . . Parents pick it up as they go along, and that's exactly the way great teachers are forged'.[8]

In the summer of 2012 Michael Gove extended the 'freedom' to hire unqualified teachers from his free school programme to the country's 1,500 academies. There is now no requirement for teachers in academies and free schools to have GCSE qualifications, let alone a degree or QTS, a crucial act of deregulation that is expected to be rolled out to all state schools at some point in the future.

The importance of qualifications has been highlighted by a number of worrying recent cases. In early 2013, Annaliese Briggs was appointed principal of Pimlico Primary, a school for 60 pupils, on the site of Pimlico

Academy, run by Lord Nash's Futures Academy charity. (Lord Nash is an Education Minister in the Lords.) Prior to taking on the job, Briggs, an English literature graduate from Queen Mary, University of London, had worked as a junior member of staff at the politically conservative think tank Civitas. She had no qualifications when appointed but was reportedly trained in Wandsworth in preparation for the beginning of the school year.[9] Briggs resigned only a few months later in October 2013. Sources close to the academy say she was finding it difficult to cope with the workload. One local teacher, who did not want to be named, said he was surprised that such an inexperienced candidate had been selected. 'She was not happy because she could not cope with the job, full stop. It was too much to learn, too quickly.'

The Discovery New School in Crawley, West Sussex, was one of the first 24 free schools to open in 2011, but was declared failing and placed in special measures by watchdog Ofsted in May. Five of the school's seven teachers were unqualified. It was ordered to close its doors in late 2013.

The UK appears to be on very weak ground compared to many high-performing nations around the world. These countries work hard to attract the best possible recruits, train them rigorously and offer qualified teachers the highest quality professional development throughout their careers. Teacher training programmes very often combine university level study, ensuring a high degree of subject knowledge, as well as a profound grasp of pedagogy, child development, and the development of research skills.

In Finland, one of the top OECD performers (according to PISA rankings released in late 2013), a highly qualified and respected teaching force lies at the heart of that country's educational success. Parents view the nation's rigorously trained teachers as professionals of the highest quality and prospective teachers regard the job as one conferring dignity and respect on them akin to other professionals such as doctors, lawyers, engineers, economists and architects.

Finnish teachers are carefully selected: only 1 in 10 applicants is successful in their application to train as a teacher. As well as taking an initial three-year degree in the subject or subjects of their choice, they do a further two-year master's degree in order to become teachers. A broad based teacher-education curriculum makes sure that 'prospective teachers develop deep professional insight into education from several perspectives, including educational psychology and sociology, curriculum theory, student assessment, special-needs education, and didactics (pedagogical content knowledge) in their selected subject areas'.[10] Those who wish to become teachers are also required to develop their own research skills to the highest academic standards and teachers are expected throughout their careers to keep up-to-date with the latest research and developments in both their own areas of subject expertise and the latest pedagogical development. They are well funded to do so.

This lengthy and detailed process of teacher education, including a long period of induction into the art of classroom practice, has several important outcomes: teaching has a high professional standing and once qualified and working within schools, individuals are trusted to work autonomously, including in terms of curriculum design and implementation. As Pasi Sahlberg notes, 'Finnish experience shows that it is more important to ensure that teachers' work in schools is based on professional dignity and social respect so that they can fulfill their intention of selecting teaching as lifetime careers'.[11]

In South Korea, where teaching is also a highly respected profession, teacher training takes place within special teachers colleges or specified universities. Programmes of study require four years of coursework, involving

Teachers don't need qualifications

both subject disciplines and general pedagogical theory. A large part of the training involves understanding of 'general pedagogy'. Students take 11 subjects, including educational psychology, educational sociology, educational philosophy and school and classroom management. In addition, they must undertake practise teaching for nine weeks and six months of post-employment training which 'involves instructional guidance and evaluation, classroom supervision and instruction on clerical work and student guidance'.

In Ontario, Canada, those wishing to be teachers complete a four-year undergraduate degree and then do a further year of teacher training. In 2012 the provincial government decided to increase teacher training by a further year (starting in 2014). They decided to do this 'given the challenges and increasing demands that teachers face'. The aim is to give more practical, in-class training for new teachers and follows years of pressure from teacher educators. In 2003, Jane Gaskell, then dean at the Ontario Institute for Studies in Education at the University of Toronto, criticised teacher training 'crammed' into the eight months in a university year, and noted that hairdressers get more training – 10 months.[12] 'We can't do it in eight months in a responsible way.'

The British government seems determined to undercut the importance not just of a qualification per se but the role of universities in teacher training. The introduction of unqualified teachers is part of a wider policy aimed at shifting teacher training from the universities to the classroom using organisations like Teach First and Schools Direct, with the latter schemes and their recruits clearly given preferential treatment in terms of funding while many of the prestigious and highly praised PGCE courses around the country are under threat.[13] University courses training the next generation of classroom teachers had their funding dramatically cut in the autumn of 2012.[14]

It is patently clear that this shift in, and shortening of, teacher instruction stems from a deep distrust of what the coalition government and its allies believes is the harmful progressivism over decades of what they like to call the 'education establishment'. As Robert Peal, author of *Progressively Worse*, recently observed, with approval, 'university education departments, the temples of progressive education, are in the process of being, if not cleansed, significantly challenged. The newly established school-centred initial teacher training schemes mean that trainee teachers can bypass the traditional university-based PGCE and train in the classroom as apprentices to experienced teachers instead. Indoctrination in child centred ways at a university department is no longer a prerequisite of becoming a qualified teacher.'[15]

But for Chris Husbands, the current director of the Institute of Education, the decision to transfer responsibility for teacher training in England away from universities to schools flies in the face of findings on best practice internationally. 'In Singapore, the government is clear: the improvements in teacher training since a low point of low morale and shortages in the 1980s have been driven by improving teacher training through the National Institute of Education,' he says. 'I was in Singapore working for the government a few weeks ago and no one could believe what we are doing in terms of de-regulation.'[16]

Such a fundamental shift in the means of provision of new recruits to the nation's classroom promotes teaching as a practical, craft-like activity rather than a profession underpinned by any form of theoretical understanding. In *Education Under Siege*, the former Director of the Institute of Education, Peter Mortimore, underlines the importance of strong background knowledge.

Topics such as how children develop/how humans learn/ how subject knowledge can be adapted for children of different ages/how pupils with special needs can best be supported/how to evaluate one's own work as a teacher, combined with awareness of the latest research on learning, and the history of education itself are best studied at university.[17]

Mortimore particularly stresses the importance of adapting expert knowledge for learners of different ages and stages.

This is something one never has to consider until one starts teaching but it is extremely challenging and takes some teachers years to get right. This means that much time (both of the new teacher and of his/ her pupils) can be saved by guidance from university experts during the teachers' training.[18]

Many other skills and kinds of knowledge are lost with non-qualified teachers, or teachers who are given a sharply reduced period of teacher education. New teachers, who are given a few weeks induction before being sent into the classroom, are unlikely to be given the chance to consider different theories of learning – and how to evaluate them. University-based teacher training enables prospective teachers to carefully evaluate all the available research and only then – if they deem it appropriate – to modify their teaching in the light of their new knowledge. A university-based training also gives trainee teachers the chance to observe practice in different – possibly contrasting – schools, before they are committed to any one institution in particular. This variety of experience gives them the opportunity to discuss contrasting professional practice with an expert teacher (from outside any of the schools in question) and is a chance to reflect on pedagogies, their respective costs and potential advantages.[19]

As the NUT point out,

The rigorous criteria involved in achieving Qualified Teacher Status (QTS) ensures that teachers possess solid knowledge and understanding of educational values and subject matter, and high standards of planning, monitoring, assessment and class management. QTS represents a formal set of skills, qualities, and professional standards that are recognised as essential aspects of an effective educator.[20]

Francis Gilbert, co-founder of the Local Schools Network, and author of several books on teaching, strongly challenges the idea that teaching is 'just about subject knowledge' added to a 'bit of craft or technique'. For him

> what goes on in the classroom is really complex and goes way beyond a set of rules or sorting out seating plans. To be a good teacher you have to really consider children as individuals, know how children learn, be in possession of a wide variety of different strategies. For instance, to know about 'multiple intelligences' is really useful.

Teaching, says Gilbert

> is about so much more than being a trained craftsman. It's about becoming a professional who must deal with a multitude of complex situations. It's about intellectual awareness as well as having all the toolkit . . . it's a mode of being.[21]

Professor Lori Beckett et al. argue that teaching is an intellectual activity which needs to be underpinned by high-quality teacher education.[22] She writes: 'A teacher who cannot or who does not wish to go on learning, will become a hindrance to the progress of education and a danger to the intellectual development of hundreds of children.' Gilbert takes this argument further with his emphasis on the importance of teachers understanding what really works in the classroom, backed up by the continuous research by experts in 'evidence-based pedagogy'.

103

He argues that it is about shifting the focus of teaching as being a means of social control to being an emancipatory activity that enables students and teachers to enjoy a measure of intellectual freedom.

> It is very different from the 'top-down' approach one saw with the National Literacy Strategies . . . we need to get every teacher reflecting deeply and seriously upon their practice, thinking hard about what is motivating children, what is helping children to learn, and what is not.[23]

Anthony Seldon praises the so-called 'dynamism' of unqualified teachers. But he was (until the summer of 2014) a headmaster of a school that charges over £30,000 a year, with small classes of highly motivated and affluent children who are themselves trained in the arts of 'emotional intelligence'. There may be room for the occasional unqualified 'dynamic' individual in such an environment (although most private schools actually employ teachers with QTS) but the challenges of the state system are far greater and more diverse in intake: an argument, surely, for even higher educational and professional standards. According to Gilbert:

> Faced with a difficult inner-city class, a trained teacher will reflect on what is happening, come up with work that meets the needs of each learner, will enter into a dialogue with students and other professionals. An untrained teacher might well resort to the idea of discipline, handing out detentions or just shouting.[24]

Unqualified teachers may also have difficulty coping with vulnerable pupils with behavioural issues and special educational needs. How can an untrained individual – however talented – learn about the disabilities, obvious and subtle, faced by so many young learners, without drawing on the serious study of experts? Whatever their subject expertise, untrained teachers lack the pedagogical background and guidance needed to maximise children's learning potential and properly support their educational development. According to one teacher who contributed to the NASUWT poll, the majority of unsatisfactory lessons at her school were taught by unqualified staff. Another said that head teachers hired unqualified staff (who are, of course, cheaper) for purely financial gain 'with no thought for the education of students'.[25]

Unlike many of the other issues touched on in this book, there is an emerging consensus against unqualified teachers in mainstream politics. In a speech in autumn 2013, Deputy Prime Minister Nick Clegg criticised the policy.

> As we move to an era of greater autonomy and schools have greater freedoms to decide things for themselves, we at the same time have to ask them to respect certain basic quality standards so that parents, regardless of where their son and daughter go to school, can be reassured that their children are going to be taught by qualified teachers [and] they are going to be taught the national curriculum like in any other schools.[26]

Labour's previous shadow education spokesperson, Tristram Hunt, has declared that 'Under Labour, all teachers will have to become qualified, teachers will be given greater opportunities to further their career progression and development and, as in other high status professions, teachers will be regularly revalidated'.[27] The recent Blunkett review on the role of a 'middle tier' in education has stated unequivocally that the Labour Party would ensure that practising teachers would either have to have, or would be in the process of gaining, qualifications. In the summer of 2014, the Labour Party also proposed the idea of 'master teachers' based on the Singaporean model.[28]

Teachers don't need qualifications

The influential group of heads, known as The Heads Roundtable, has proposed that,

> In order to improve the quality of teaching and increase the attractiveness of the profession to our best graduates, schools, in partnership with Initial Teacher Education providers, will deliver a two-year Induction Programme for all entrants to the teaching profession with a five-year pathway to a Professional Qualification with Masters Degree Equivalence.[29]

They also want to see a teacher-run and teacher-led College of Teaching, with 'improving pedagogy [as] its core purpose . . . It will be the main body to represent the profession, independent of government, setting standards for teachers based upon on-going research into effective practice. We need to develop a professional culture where all teachers are continually refining their teaching skills'.[30]

Experts such as Peter Mortimore believe that ministers should 'be looking for ways *to increase the length of the PGCE rather than abolish it.* Surely, the reality is that education ministers (of all parties) resent the existence of expertise outside of their control. Hence they want to discourage new teachers from being critical – a characteristic likely to be nurtured by the experts who, having spent years learning to be good teachers and then extended their skills with a PhD and doing research will provide models for the trainee teachers'.[31]

The evidence of almost all the experts is, then, clearly in favour of well-qualified teachers, with access to continuing and meaningful professional development. The restoration of a robust teacher qualification, freed from outside political interference, appears to be popular with parents from across the political spectrum and those who support all kinds of schools. According to a survey conducted by Opinium for the New Schools Network, the body charged with promoting free schools, even those who 'give tentative support' to the idea of free schools are worried about the introduction of untrained teachers. Some of the detail of the policy is met by worry rather than support. A key plank of the present free school policy is that they can employ teaching staff that do not have a PGCE. A clear majority (60 per cent) say they are concerned that free schools are able to hire unqualified teachers, with only 30 per cent not concerned. Even Conservative voters are more concerned than not (52 per cent to 39 per cent).[32]

According to the NUT-commissioned You Gov survey of parents' views on education, the overwhelming majority of parents (89 per cent) do not want their children to attend schools where teachers do not have professional teaching qualifications. Only 1 per cent of parents felt comfortable with unqualified teachers taking charge of a class. The vast majority believe that employing unqualified teaching staff in free schools was designed to save money, not improve standards.[33]

Notes

1 https://mckinseyonsociety.com/how-the-worlds-best-performing-schools-come-out-on-top/ accessed 28 January 2015.

2 Pasi Sahlberg, *Finnish lessons: What can the world learn from educational change in Finland?* Teachers College Press, 2011, p. 70.

3 Download table 4 here, https://www.gov.uk/government/publications/school-workforce-in-england-november-2013 accessed 28 January 2015.

4 http://www.jobsgopublic.com/jobs/unqualified-teacher-of-maths-x-2-n-a/from/ysb5zvlipqcho/334/of/1041/opening_at/desc accessed 28 January 2015.

5 http://www.theguardian.com/education/2013/mar/31/schools-hiring-unqualified-teachers-money accessed 28 January 2015.

6 http://www.tes.co.uk/article.aspx?storycode=6064221 accessed 28 January 2015.

7 http://www.theguardian.com/education/mortarboard/2010/may/17/nick-gibb-upsets-teachers accessed 28 January 2015.

8 http://www.theguardian.com/commentisfree/2013/oct/28/teaching-qualification-nick-clegg-course accessed 28 January 2015.

9 http://www.theguardian.com/education/2013/oct/09/free-school-head-no-teaching-qualifications-leaves-job accessed 28 January 2015.

Teachers don't need qualifications

10 Pasi Sahlberg, *Finnish lessons: What can the world learn from educational change in Finland?* Teachers College Press, 2011, p. 80.
11 Pasi Sahlberg, *Finnish lessons: What can the world learn from educational change in Finland?* Teachers College Press, 2011, p. 70.
12 http://www.thestar.com/news/canada/2012/03/22/ontario_to_increase_teacher_training_to_two_years.html accessed 28 January 2015.
13 Harris, R. and Crolla, C. Teach first shouldn't get preferential treatment http://www.localschoolsnetwork.org.uk/2014/06/teach-first-shouldnt-get-preferential-treatment/ accessed 28 January 2015.
14 http://www.theguardian.com/education/2013/apr/29/teacher-training-universities-schools-direct accessed 28 January 2015.
15 Robert Peal, *Progressively Worse*, Civitas, 2014.
16 http://www.theguardian.com/education/2014/jan/14/universities-best-place-to-train-teachers-report-says?CMP=twt_gu accessed 28 January 2015.
17 Peter Mortimore, *Education Under Siege*, Polity Press, p. 55.
18 Private correspondence with Peter Mortimore.
19 I am grateful to Peter Mortimore for pointing out many of these valuable elements of a university-based teacher training course and which now risk being lost.
20 https://www.teachers.org.uk/edufacts/qualified-teacher-status accessed 17 August 2015.
21 Francis Gilbert in private conversation.
22 Ed Beckett, *Teacher education through active engagement: Raising the professional voice*, Routledge, 2013.
23 http://www.francisgilbert.co.uk/2014/03/can-evidence-based-pedagogy-raise-levels-of-achievement/ accessed 28 January 2015.
24 Francis Gilbert in private conversation.
25 http://www.theguardian.com/education/2013/mar/31/schools-hiring-unqualified-teachers-money accessed 28 January 2015.
26 http://www.theguardian.com/politics/2013/oct/20/nick-clegg-david-laws-free-schools accessed 28 January 2015.
27 http://press.labour.org.uk/post/73353035764/labour-will-reverse-david-camerons-downgrading-of accessed 17 August 2015.
28 http://www.theguardian.com/education/2014/jul/05/master-teachers-labour-education-tristram-hunt accessed 28 January 2015.
29 https://headteachersroundtable.files.wordpress.com/2014/05/headteachers-roundtable-education-election-manifesto-2015.pdf (p. 5), accessed 17 August 2015.
30 https://headteachersroundtable.files.wordpress.com/2014/05/headteachers-roundtable-education-election-manifesto-2015.pdf accessed 28 January 2015.
31 Private correspondence with Peter Mortimore.
32 http://news.opinium.co.uk/survey-results/free-schools-get-reserved-support accessed 28 January 2015.
33 http://www.teachers.org.uk/node/17949 accessed 28 January 2015.

Private schools have the magic DNA

We are used to the dramatic newspaper claims – some facts emphasised by CAPITAL LETTERS just in case we should miss the POINT. 'Private pupils are SIX TIMES more likely to get A* grades at GCSEs than those at state schools.'[1] Or 'A third of private pupils score 3 A* grades at A level . . . compared to one in TEN at state schools'.[2] It is a superiority of performance, we are again told, that extends into higher education.

> Private schools educate only 7 per cent of the population, their students take up almost half the places at Oxbridge and one-third of the places across the whole Russell Group. According to the education charity the Sutton Trust, an independent day school student is 55 times more likely to win a place at Oxbridge and 22 times more likely to go to a top-ranked university than a state school student from a poor household. It is not just education that the parental cheque book buys but the assumption of a substantial socio-economic premium.[3]

It is no surprise then to come across an article, even in a liberal broadsheet, declaring 'The awful truth: to get ahead you need a private education'.[4]

Such, then, is the assumed and endlessly celebrated power of private schools in the early twenty-first century, that politicians increasingly turn to the independent schools to ask them to lend the 'secrets' of their success to thousands of the nation's hard-pressed state schools. In a speech in February 2013 former Secretary of State Michael Gove argued that that 'he wanted to push state schools further so that they would become indistinguishable from private schools' with longer hours, more after-school activities and testing. State school pupils, he suggested, should even be entered for the 'common entrance' exam taken by 13-year-olds in some private schools.[5]

But what is this unique private school DNA? Is it really, as Lord Adonis, the former Labour minister asserts, down to the fact that independent schools are run by charitable trusts, free from the taint of meddling local authorities? (See Chapter 2 for myth-busting on this issue.) Or could it be because private schools are able to hire unqualified teachers, timetable a longer day, enjoy extra curricula activities or operate some kind of house system?

Of course, many state schools already enjoy rich extra-curricula programmes, operate a longer school day or employ versions of the house system. Government interference, including a national curriculum, league tables and other accountability measures, hinder the freedoms they might otherwise enjoy. For all that, there remain two substantive reasons why private schools confer such a great advantage on those who go to them.

First, most private schools enjoy superior, and often lavish, resources compared to the majority of state schools. At the top end of the market, public schools like Eton, Harrow and Winchester charge average fees of £33,400 plus a year while the family of a pupil at private day schools will pay, on average, £11,500 rising to £15,000 in London. In comparison, state schools spend between £3,000 to £8,000 per pupil per year.

According to the head teacher of one of the most expensive day schools in the country such are the current costs that 'middle-class families' are being priced out of private education. Andrew Halls, the head teacher of King's College School in Wimbledon, south west London, claimed that 'local lawyers, accountants and military officers had stopped sending their children to [his] school because of the costs' and that in many areas private schools had merely become 'finishing schools for the children of oligarchs'.[6]

As David and George Kynaston point out in a recent article in the *New Statesman*, such high figures are not ones that

> the average household – disposable income of approximately £25,000 – can afford. If you are in a position to pay fees or even a substantial portion of fees, you are far removed from the reality of most parents and are paying to confer an advantage on your child that very few can afford.[7]

Students at Wellington College, for example, a top boarding public school with fees currently at around £33,000 a year, enjoy access to no fewer than sixteen rugby pitches, two floodlit astroturf pitches, a state-of-the art sports hall, twenty-two hard tennis courts, twelve cricket pitches, an athletics track, two lacrosse pitches, six netball courts, a shooting range, a nine-hole golf course, six art studios, its own section on the Saatchi website, a theatre and TV crew, a professional recording studio for aspiring musicians and a number of concert venues. As journalist Peter Wilby argued, students at Marlborough College enjoy a 'variety of facilities which, if extended to every state school, would require (according to one calculation) 33m acres, or more than half the English countryside'.[8] Even less well-resourced private schools have superior sports and cultural facilities to the most well-endowed state schools.

Private schools have the magic DNA

In current educational debate, the issue of class sizes in state schools has taken a back seat, with some arguing that it makes little, or no, difference to successful educational outcomes.[9] Yet for many parents, and leaders, of private schools, small class sizes, a higher teacher–pupil ratio, and all the related advantages that come it, are clearly very important. OECD studies show that class sizes in UK state secondary schools are on average more than double those in independent schools – 21.1 compared with 10.1. Since 2010, and squeezes on the education budget, the pupil teacher ratio has risen.[10] [11] As one teacher and private school parent put it,

> I've taught classes with 15 pupils and classes with 35. Children in smaller classes feel more confident about contributing and I had more time for them. I knew the name of every pupil in the school; I felt part of a close knit community and so did they.[12]

Since the 1970s private school teacher numbers have doubled relative to state schools: a seventh of England's teaching force is now in private schools, a far higher proportion of teachers with better and higher degrees, including some who first enter teaching via the Teach First scheme – a recruitment scheme specifically designed to improve teaching in the most disadvantaged state schools.

But it is not just first-rate resources and small classes that help some private schools succeed. The vast majority of children in private education, including many of the supposed 'disadvantaged' – that is, those who are in receipt of bursaries and scholarships – come from relatively affluent homes. Although 33.7 per cent of pupils at private schools receive help with their fees, two thirds of these are either reductions for military, clergy, siblings and staff, or scholarships and then only for part fees.[13] On average only one in 12 private school students receives a means-tested bursary.

Historian David Kynaston recently probed these figures in greater detail. After managing to

> deconstruct the somewhat opaque census figures
> for the 1,223 members of the Independent Schools
> Council . . . we found that although one-third of pupils
> at private schools receive help with their fees, averaging
> about a quarter, those pupils are often siblings of other
> pupils and/or the children of staff or the military or
> the clergy; that one in 12 private-school pupils receive
> a means-tested bursary, but two-thirds of those one
> in 12 are still paying more than half; and finally, that
> fewer than one in 100 pupils are in receipt of a full bur-
> sary, i.e. paying no fees. In short, we found that most
> parents going down the private-school route still pay
> heavily to do so – and that the fees they pay are out of
> reach of the population as a whole.[14]

Private schools, then, are made up from children largely
from relatively well-off homes where education is valued
and learning can be supported by parents and the wider
family. Put such children in a relatively, and often magnifi-
cently, advantaged educational setting and it is no surprise
that educational outcomes will soar. By definition, private
schools face none of the tough challenges of the generally
under-resourced state sector, particularly in poorer areas,
where many school leaders are dealing with chronic problems from buildings in poor disrepair to high levels of
parental disengagement and tired and demoralised teachers.

However, private schools are not, it seems, better at
educating their pupils than the state sector. According to
Professor Ron Glatter,

> In spite of these great advantages there is room for doubt
> about the educational superiority of our private schools.
> One little reported finding from the PISA results was
> that once account has been taken of the socio-economic

background of pupils, state schools in the UK outperform private schools by a considerable margin.[15]

This suggests two things: first, that many state schools are doing an excellent job in often highly adverse circumstances and second, that much of the 'success' of our private schools can be attributed, as already argued, to the alchemy of resources combined with the socially and culturally advantaged nature of their intake. Yet this highly significant finding has been almost entirely overlooked in public discussion about this topic.[16]

According to inspection data from Ofsted, 69 per cent of non-affiliated private schools inspected under the old framework from September 2012 and 31 December 2012 were good or better and 31 per cent were judged 'less than good'. Sixty-four per cent of private schools inspected under the new framework from 1 January 2013 to 31 August 2013 were 'Good' or better; 36 per cent were 'Less than Good' and 13 per cent were 'Inadequate'. For state schools inspected between 1 September 2012 and 31 August 2013 under the old and new framework: 64 per cent were 'Good' or better: 30 per cent 'Required Improvement' and six per cent were 'Inadequate'.

OECD surveys confirm that while those who attend private schools tend to perform significantly better in PISA tests, pupils in state schools with a similar socio-economic background as private schools tend to achieve the same results.[17]

Indeed, many on the political right now acknowledge that, in many cases, state schools outperform private schools when it comes to the quality of their teaching and leadership. Sam Freedman, former adviser to Michael Gove at the DfE, writing in *The Guardian* about why state schools don't need the private sector's advice, said,

while there are great practitioners in both sectors, teaching well in comprehensives requires a different level of persistence, commitment and skill. Classes are much larger and the ability range is typically much wider. The quality of teaching and leadership I've seen in our best inner-city state schools, such as Westminster Academy and Mulberry school in Tower Hamlets . . . is world-class and would, frankly, be wasted in the private sector.

Later in the same article, Freedman refers to 'a widespread and inaccurate belief in the innate superiority of private schools when we should be looking to build on success in the state system'.[18]

How then can private schools, with their superior resources and selective intake but no better performance magically transform a state sector that must by definition educate all children from all social backgrounds and across a wider ability range?

In previous decades, private schools have been asked to open themselves up to poorer students through selective bursaries (a scheme that never really took off) and the promotion of 'assisted places' – the latter abolished by the incoming Labour government in 1997. The generous tax breaks granted to the private sector, worth about a hundred million a year, is another tool used by government to compel schools to open up their facilities to local students, the so-called 'public benefit' tests which has, again, had mixed results.[19] In December 2014, Tristram Hunt, Shadow Secretary of Education, announced that Labour in government would 'introduce a school partnership standard requiring all private schools to form genuine and accountable partnerships with state schools if they want to keep their business rates relief'. This penalty was estimated to be worth around 147 million a year.[20] Hunt argued that 'Britain will only thrive in the 21st century on the back of an education system where pupils enjoy equality of opportunity. This crippling public–private impasse has gone on too long.'[21]

Private schools have the magic DNA

Hunt's proposal is a more radical version of some of the new strategies that have emerged in recent years, first under new Labour and more recently under the coalition, that aim to bridge the historic divide between private/public education sectors.[22] Ministers have asked private schools to get involved more directly in state education – principally through partnering with or sponsoring some of the 'new' academies. Private schools that have played some part in this programme include Brighton College, Dulwich, Eton, Highgate, King's Canterbury, Malvern, Marlborough, Oundle, Sevenoaks, Winchester and Uppingham.

Many of these independent schools have since withdrawn from the scheme, citing social and economic challenges that they cannot overcome. Dulwich School has pulled out its involvement in the Isle of Sheppey academy on the grounds that 'You need people who have a lot of maintained sector experience to actually come and work on the Isle of Sheppey'.[23] And Wellington College, headed by Anthony Seldon, which formed a close partnership with an academy, has had many well-publicised troubles with exam results, staffing issues and even, it is reported, control of assemblies at its sponsored academy.[24]

Some private school heads honestly acknowledge that they are not up to the challenge. Jon Coles, the chief executive of United Learning, which runs both private and state schools, has admitted the difficulties: 'The truth is that not all that many of our independent school heads would be great heads of challenging academies.' He quoted one of his private school heads: 'I take my hat off to these guys who run academies. I wouldn't last five minutes in that environment.'[25]

On a slightly different note, there has been rising opposition, from within the independent sector, to the sponsorship programme. At the Girls' Schools Association annual conference in November 2013, its then-president Louise Robinson said it was 'beyond the pale' to expect hard-up families to pay for a private education only to see the cash spent on the 'local competition'.[26] A similar challenge has come from the Independent Association of Prep Schools, which represents 600 (often small) institutions educating under-13s. David Hanson, its chief executive, said that asking these schools to get involved was 'wrongheaded', not least because they lack the 'capacity or the means to sponsor an academy'.[27]

A second strategy, aimed at breaking down the so-called 'Berlin Wall' between the two sectors, encourages the conversion of private schools into state schools via the free school and academy programme. More than a hundred private schools are predicted to make the move into the state sector in the next decade according to former Schools Minister Lord Adonis.[28]

But who really benefits? The barely reported truth here is that nearly all the schools choosing to opt in are failing according to the market principles advocated by successive government as the solution to the problems of state education. Many simply can't attract enough pupils. Given that it has been argued that failing state schools should shrink and close, why should the same principles not be applied to fragile institutions within the private sector?

More worryingly, private schools converting to academy/free school status can take advantage of the private contracts drawn up between Secretary of State and individual schools to vary schools' admissions arrangements in their favour. For example, the Belvedere Academy in Liverpool, which converted to a state-funded school almost ten years ago, was given permission to continue prioritising applications from pupils at its fee-paying Junior School, and is now ranked as one of England's most socially segregated schools: fifth out of 3,323.[29]

If every former private school were to operate in this manner it is easy to see, as Fiona Millar has argued, how a 'self-perpetuating virtuous circle of aspirant, affluent pupils may sustain league table positions for years to come . . . A new type of elite school, funded by taxpayer, will have taken root.'³⁰

But is a private education really that desirable? While comprehensive schools are, by definition, dealing with children across the ability range, it remains perfectly possible for a hard-working student to attend almost any state school in the country and secure excellent results, a place at a good university, and a successful job.

In addition, despite their much-feted advantages, a private education may well contain significant disbenefits. As Lord Adonis said to the HMC last year, 'private schools have created a world apart for many students, as social segregation has got worse'. He went on to point out that pupils at private schools meet only children from the same background.

> It is seriously disabling for students going to exclusive fee-paying schools that they see so little of society. They mix in a very narrow social medium. They don't for the most part meet the most of the rest of society, including those who don't have parents of substantial means. If what we want is a one nation society, it is not good for them and it is not good for wider society.³¹

Or as one 'escapee from one such institution' wrote to the letters page of *The Guardian* in 2011:

> my experience is that the ethos . . . instilled [. . .] largely consists of overweening arrogance, a total inability to admit errors and a feeling of innate superiority to the rest of the population, leading to such joyous public-school-led adventures as the Iraq war and the banking crisis.³²

Private schools are not superior to state schools. They are more privileged institutions educating the most privileged children in our society; it is their occasional failure that is remarkable, not their manifest advantages. For all this, even some of the most ardent supporters of private education are now re-thinking the advantages of a fee paying sector. In a piece entitled 'It's official – private schools are a waste of money' free school founder Toby Young argued that the salary premium that allegedly attaches to a private education will be more than wiped out by the fees.

> That is to say, if you take two children from identical backgrounds and with exactly the same level of intelligence and send one to a private school and the other to a state school, the one educated privately will earn £57,653 more between the ages of 26 and 42 than the one who went to a state school. That's an average pay difference of £3,600 a year, which is considerably less than the average private school fees – £12,153 for a day school and £27,600 for a boarding school. Even if you send your child to a day school for seven years, the cumulative cost will be £85,071. So it's official. Educating your child at a private school is a waste of money – a colossal waste of money if you send them to a boarding school.[33]

Even *Tatler*, the magazine of the affluent, suggests that private education could now be a waste of money. In a special feature on the 'best state schools', published in early 2014, the magazine claimed that

> to put two children through the private system costs around £600,000 – that's £1.2 million before tax. And is private really superior? Not always, not any more. The state sector has some spanking-new buildings, strong discipline, sporting rigour and academic ambition. Plus, your child gets a better preparation for the real world, the one where not everything is handed to them

on a sterling-silver platter, where there is a cosmopolitan mix, where you will have to fight to get to the top.[34]

But given the consolidation of very tangible private school privilege in recent years, more substantive and genuinely radical proposals are now being put forward. In December 2014, after examining in forensic detail the ways in which private schools hinder genuine equal opportunity for the majority of families, writer and historian David Kynaston, no enemy of 'institutions of proven academic excellence', argued that

> ultimately there may be no alternative to full integration into the national educational system – a system now allowing significantly more operational autonomy within it than 10 or 20 years ago . . . Fundamentally, my problem is with the fee-paying principle – which leads directly to engines of privilege, blocks relative social mobility and perpetuates a Berlin Wall not just in our education system but in our society.[35]

Notes

1 http://www.dailymail.co.uk/news/article-2033314/Private-pupils-SIX-TIMES-likely-A-grades-GCSEs-state-schools.html accessed 28 January 2015.
2 http://www.dailymail.co.uk/news/article-2051335/A-levels-Third-private-pupils-3-A-grades-1-10-state-schools.html accessed 28 January 2015.
3 http://www.newstatesman.com/2014/01/education-private-schools-berlin-wall accessed 28 January 2015.
4 http://www.theguardian.com/politics/2010/may/02/private-education-leaders-debate-parliament accessed 28 January 2015.
5 http://www.bbc.co.uk/news/education-26015535 accessed 28 January 2015.
6 http://www.thetimes.co.uk/tto/education/article4275765.ece accessed 28 January 2015.
7 http://www.newstatesman.com/2014/01/education-private-schools-berlin-wall accessed 28 January 2015.
8 http://www.theguardian.com/commentisfree/2014/feb/03/state-schools-independents-michael-gove accessed 28 January 2015.

9 https://www.youtube.com/watch?v=qGnbcMOKtQQ accessed 28 January 2015.
10 http://www.theguardian.com/teacher-network/teacher-blog/2013/jul/04/education-private-transform-state-schools accessed 28 January 2015.
11 http://www.andrewdismore.org.uk/home/2014/06/13/conservatives-break-promise-on-smaller-class-sizes-as-the-number-of-infants-taught-in-large-classes-soars/ accessed 28 January 2015.
12 http://www.parentdish.co.uk/teen/why-private-schools-are-better-than-state/ accessed 28 January 2015.
13 http://www.newstatesman.com/2014/01/education-private-schools-berlin-wall accessed 28 January 2015.
14 http://www.theguardian.com/books/2014/dec/05/-sp-social-mobility-decline-elitist-education-david-kynaston accessed 28 January 2015.
15 http://www.oecd.org/pisa/46624007.pdf accessed 28 January 2015.
16 http://www.theguardian.com/teacher-network/teacher-blog/2013/jul/04/education-private-transform-state-schools accessed 28 January 2015.
17 http://www.oecd.org/pisa/pisaproducts/pisainfocus/48482894.pdf accessed 28 January 2015.
18 http://www.theguardian.com/commentisfree/2014/nov/30/state-schools-dont-need-private-sector-advice-public-schools accessed 28 January 2015.
19 http://news.tes.co.uk/b/news/2013/10/04/leading-independent-school-pulls-out-of-academy-sponsorship.aspx accessed 28 January 2015.
20 http://academiesweek.co.uk/what-is-tristram-hunts-private-school-tax-plan/ accessed 28 January 2015.
21 quoted in: http://www.theguardian.com/books/2014/dec/05/-sp-social-mobility-decline-elitist-education-david-kynaston accessed 28 January 2015.
22 http://webarchive.nationalarchives.gov.uk/20141124154759/http://www.ofsted.gov.uk/resources/independentstate-school-partnerships accessed 28 January 2015.
23 https://news.tes.co.uk/b/news/2013/10/04/leading-independent-school-pulls-out-of-academy-sponsorship.aspx accessed 28 January 2015.
24 http://www.theguardian.com/education/2013/oct/22/private-school-head-runs-state-school accessed 28 January 2015.
25 http://www.theguardian.com/commentisfree/2014/nov/30/state-schools-dont-need-private-sector-advice-public-schools accessed 28 January 2015.
26 http://www.dailymail.co.uk/news/article-2235499/We-shouldnt-open-facilities-state-pupils-insists-private-schools-chief.html accessed 28 January 2015.

Private schools have the magic DNA

27 http://www.parentsoutloud.com/mr-gove-has-missed-the-point-over-criticisms-of-academy-sponsorship/#sthash.9fhkhpNO.dpbs accessed 28 January 2015.

28 http://www.independent.co.uk/news/education/schools/as-many-as-100-independent-schools-could-join-the-state-sector-within-a-decade-as-free-schools-or-academies-9077705.html accessed 28 January 2015.

29 http://fairadmissions.org.uk/map/ accessed 28 January 2015.

30 http://www.theguardian.com/education/2014/feb/11/private-schools-enter-state-sector accessed 28 January 2015.

31 http://andrewadonis.com/2013/05/10/pupils-%E2%80%98segregated-from-society%E2%80%99-by-exclusive-private-schools/ accessed 28 January 2015.

32 http://www.theguardian.com/education/2011/sep/04/questions-of-character-building accessed 28 January 2015.

33 http://blogs.telegraph.co.uk/news/tobyyoung/100278503/its-official-private-schools-are-a-waste-of-money/ accessed 28 January 2015.

34 http://www.tatler.com/news/articles/january-2014/the-tatler-guide-to-state-schools—part-one accessed 28 January 2015.

35 http://www.theguardian.com/books/2014/dec/05/-sp-social-mobility-decline-elitist-education-david-kynaston accessed 28 January 2015.

Progressive education lowers standards

In a speech delivered to the Social Market Foundation in early 2013, former Education Secretary Michael Gove made an extraordinary claim. Over the past half century, he said, England's state schools have been in the grip of a

> Progressive educational theory [that] sought to replace an emphasis on acquiring knowledge in traditional subjects with a new stress on children following where their curiosity led them. *And that was usually away from outdated practices such as reading, writing and arithmetic.*[1]

Welcome to our final myth: that most of the country's schools are in the grip of progressive educators actively working to drive down pupil achievement. This is, in fact, a very old argument – but one given fresh political energy and apparent credibility by an alliance of Conservative politicians, right-leaning think tanks and idealistic young teachers, vocally disillusioned at the state of state education and supremely confident that they alone grasp the means to fix it.

Robert Peal, author of the polemic *Progressively worse: The burden of bad ideas in British schools*, who began teaching in 2011, states the modern conservative case with typical baldness, 'Progressive education has given us decades of chaotic schools, disenchanted teachers and pupil failure. Today, its legacy in Britain is an estimated seven million illiterate adults spanning the generations'.[2] At another point, Peal blithely asserts that 'Hard work is not a fashionable concept in today's schools'.[3]

While Peal acknowledges that 'Progressive education in the state sector . . . cannot be boiled down to an institution, a list of practices or even a set of clearly-defined ideas'[4] such evangelists are keen to rout out any idea or method that possibly reeks of the problem and replace it with tried-and-tested traditionalist methods. The coalition government has backed this approach with a series of policies that aim to undercut what it calls 'the education establishment' – known colloquially as The Blob – from the abolition of the 'soft' elements of public exams to a new, more supposedly 'rigorous' curriculum, to harsher forms of school accountability.

But are the claims of the new 'educational conservatives' accurate? What is their evidence base? Are our schools in the grip of some wild, radical ideology that actively prevents learning? Could other factors such as social inequality, the school structures that reflect them and persistent underfunding, and demoralisation, of state education have played any part in the poorer opportunities of poorer students? Is Ofsted really in the grip of The Blob, obsessed with soft skills not hard knowledge? And could a return to traditionalist teaching, military-style discipline and the continuing relentless attack on more innovative educational approaches harm, not help, the learning of millions of students – and so risk lowering the very standards it aims to raise?

Michael Gove is not the first public figure to attack 'progressive education' and its impact on English schools. As the blogger and teacher Andrew Old rightly points out in his introduction to Robert Peal's book 'almost all the arguments described here have been part of the history of our education system for more than five decades'.[5] In the late 1960s, the 'Black Papers', a series of interventions from conservative writers and educationists savaged the developing movement for comprehensive reform and 'child-centred' teaching as the root of all the nation's educational problems. In October 1976, in his famous 'Ruskin speech', Labour Prime Minister Jim Callaghan spoke of an 'unease felt by parents and others about the new informal methods . . . which seem to produce excellent results when they are in well-qualified hands, but are much more dubious when they are not'.[6] Modern-day Labour figures like former Schools Minister Andrew Adonis have argued strongly for a 'grammar style' academic education in all-ability state schools. But it was during his tenure that the boom in alternative, non-GCSE, vocational examinations took place.

Today's critics return to four key themes. In their view: progressive education is wedded to child-centred methods of teaching; does not believe that knowledge is central to education; is unconcerned about discipline; and holds to the ultimately defeatist view that a child's social background determines their educational and life course.[7] (For further discussion of the fallibility of over-simplified social mobility arguments, see Chapter 1.)

In *Seven myths about education*, Daisy Christodoulou, another Teach First graduate, who now works for the powerful educational chain ARK, draws heavily on Ofsted reports and her own relatively short experience of teaching to present a supposedly damning picture of a school system that fails to provide children with basic knowledge, one in which teacher-led instruction has been sidelined, with the collusion of Ofsted, in favour of amorphous project work, useless skill-building and a misplaced faith in the power of Google. In her writing, says one critic, she

125

Progressive education lowers standards

'seeks to apply the kind of tactics that Sir Arthur Harris pioneered in the art of aerial bombardment'.[8]

Robert Peal makes the extraordinary claim that progressive educators display a 'contempt for the accumulated knowledge of mankind . . . [an attitude] likely to work only to deprive the disadvantaged and excluded of an asset that will remain the exclusive property of the privileged and powerful'.[9] Peal also bemoans what he sees as widespread ill-discipline in England's schools: a message apparently underlined by the front cover of his own book, showing a group of boys fighting. (Of course, it's entirely possible that the boys are successfully enacting a scene from Shakespeare.)

For free school founder and public provocateur, Toby Young, writing in his latest work *Prisoners of the Blob: Why most educational experts are wrong about almost everything* . . . nearly everyone in [the 'education establishment'] shares the same progressive educational philosophy [namely that] skills like

> 'problem-solving' and 'critical thinking' are more important than subject knowledge . . . education should be 'child-centred' rather than 'didactic' or 'teacher-led' . . . 'group work' and 'independent learning' are superior to 'direct instruction'; that the way to interest children in a subject is to make it 'relevant'; that 'rote-learning' and 'regurgitating facts' is bad, along with discipline, hierarchy, routine and anything else that involves treating the teacher as an authority figure. The list goes on.[10]

In short, theirs is a message of gloom and doom, designed to fill every parent with horror and deep mistrust of contemporary state education, part of the modus operandi of the current GERM lobby (see Chapter 3). Such is the ferocity of the attack that it has now expanded beyond the usual targets – university education departments, the trades unions and local authorities – to take in Ofsted itself. The think tank Civitas (which publishes Young and Peal and was the first publisher of Christodoulou's book) believes that Ofsted is in the grip of the progressives, and should be reformed or scrapped because too many of its 'inspectors [are] committed to the now-discredited child-led methods of the 1960s and hostile to more-modern teacher-led approaches'.[11]

But the new anti-progressive orthodoxy is itself based on a significant absence of evidence, discernible contradictions and dubious claims. None of the new traditionalists acknowledge the major role of structural inequalities in society or the school system – from increasing social inequality to the divisive impact of private or selective education – in damaging the educational achievement of millions of children from lower-income backgrounds over several decades. Peal at least makes passing reference to the chronic underfunding of education, not to mention madcap voucher schemes, of the Thatcher years (1979–1997) that left state education in such a parlous state by the late 1990s.

Like Christodoulou, Peal frequently invokes the writing of radical thinkers from John Dewey to Robin Pedley yet severely underplays and, at times, misrepresents the complexity, nuance and tone of their work. He invokes the radical methods of A. S. Neill, founder and first head teacher of the independent co-educational boarding school Summerhill, set up in 1921, and the anarchic practices of a single London primary school, William Tyndale, in the 1970s when neither – and particularly not the latter, widely condemned at the time – are considered of relevance to contemporary classroom practice by the majority of teaching professionals. Christodoulou is highly critical of the work of philosophers such as Rousseau, Dewey and Freire, all of whom, according to experienced teacher Debra Kidd, need to be understood within a particular context.

Progressive education lowers standards

As Kidd argues,

> Dewey, for example, was responding to an education system in which children were not viewed as individuals, and where cruel forms of corporal punishment were routinely administered . . . For all three of these 'pernicious' writers, the main concern was not with facts, but with power. Each tried to assert the importance of seeing each child as a complex and capable individual. For Dewey, the child 'excels in complexity and minuteness of differentiations' so that 'one who executes the wish of others . . . is doomed to act along lines predetermined to regularity'.
>
> It is not facts he is opposed to, but the failure of the education system to value individuality. For Freire, writing in times of extreme social oppression in Brazil and Rousseau against the backdrop of the grave inequalities of the 18th century, the importance was to cast light on the plight of the poor; to try to value their lives and to build education which was holistic in nature. We cannot take their words and ideas and ridicule them with a 21st century perspective without considering the contexts in which they were written. It would be like saying that because the Romantic poets were heavily influenced by Rousseau, we should ignore their work, rooted as it is in a 'one life' philosophy. Coleridge, Wordsworth and Shelley are suddenly 'defunct' and 'pernicious'?[12]

Distortion of the past is a vital part of the new traditionalists' political arsenal. In his February 2013 Social Market Foundation speech Michael Gove asserted that 'since 1967 and the publication of the Plowden Report – the new educational orthodoxy was progressive . . . Didactic became a pejorative term'.[13] Not so, argues Professor Robin Alexander, curriculum expert and chair of the Cambridge Primary Review.

Although [Plowden] argued for children to be helped to cross subject boundaries in pursuit of knowledge and understanding, Plowden actually favoured a measured progression from a relatively open curriculum in the early years to a subject-differentiated one by age 12 – hardly revolutionary – and its discussion of curriculum was in other respects pretty conventional, using all the familiar subject names.[14]

Another claim made by Gove is that, under Plowden, 'The role – and authority – of the teacher . . . was undermined . . . The teacher was demoted from being "the sage on the stage" to a "guide by the side".'[15] Again, Alexander offers a factually based rebuttal: 'Plowden was . . . ridiculed by the demonisers for saying that all teaching, even in large classes where this was clearly impossible, should be individualised. In fact, while Plowden "*welcomed* the trend towards individual learning" it actually *recommended* "a combination of individual, group and class work".'[16] Yet Peal himself quotes from a 1978 HMI report into primary education that acknowledges that three-quarters of teachers employed a 'mainly didactic' approach and only one in twenty relied exclusively on 'exploratory methods'.[17]

As we saw in Chapter 1, belief in a common curriculum was one of the original aims of the comprehensive reform movement, and it is simply inaccurate to argue that these same reformers were anti-knowledge.[18] However, many in that early reform movement did believe that education was about more than didactic (and dull) methods of classroom teaching and that the motivation and experience of the learner was an important factor in educational success. This could be called 'child-centred'; it could also be called plain common sense.

Experienced teachers challenge the sweeping claims of the new young traditionalists. Writing in the TES, leading independent school teacher Kevin Stannard queries the new orthodoxy, asking 'is project-based learning really always bad? Do all proponents of learning by enquiry really believe that the transmission of facts has no place, ever?'[19] Headteacher Tom Sherrington rejects Christodoulou's characterisation of what goes on in today's classrooms,

> Most teachers already explicitly teach facts and transmit knowledge as part and parcel of their everyday work. If anything, we have a strong orientation towards exam preparation; exams are not as content free as some people suggest . . . school curricula are knowledge rich.[20]

Debra Kidd is critical of Christodoulou's

> over reliance on Ofsted reports . . . I am concerned at the huge leaps of assumption made from the reading of these reports into what constitutes 'good' and 'bad' teaching. For example, Christodoulou cites several tasks as evidence of dumbing down. One of these is an account of a lesson in which children wrote letters to their headteacher about uniform. It is assumed that this offers an example of learning which is content free. But without sight of those letters we cannot know.[21]

For Sherrington, good teaching depends on a mix of approaches.

> For me, after 25 years in various schools, I'm pretty clear that direct instruction and group work are as inseparable as knowledge and skills. They co-exist in a typical flow of lessons and I think it's a mistake to create a dichotomy . . . Many of the best lessons I have seen have been intensely knowledge rich but involved group work, collaborative learning and student-led activity. I have also seen numerous masterclasses of direct instruction – always, without exception, accompanied

by expert questioning and feedback. Knowledge transmission is a very limiting and limited view of teaching . . . because students always bring their perspective, their own starting point, their own ideas.[22]

For Sherrington then, the problem facing state schools is not a lack of concern for knowledge but the means to make facts stick:

> Mostly the issues are around poor behaviour, an inability to hold a class's attention, weak subject knowledge, an awkward or excessively dull expositional style, low expectations . . . all these teachers were desperately trying to transmit knowledge but failing to do so effectively.

One of the most influential voices in the debate in the US and here is American educationalist E. D. Hirsch. Hirsch believes that schools should teach a highly specific curriculum on the grounds that 'We will achieve a just and prosperous society only when our schools ensure that everyone commands enough shared knowledge to communicate effectively with everyone else'.[23] Hirsch's arguments have impressed progressives and traditionalists alike, but have largely been deployed over recent years by traditionalists. (Coalition Schools Minister, Nick Gibb, was said to keep a copy of Hirsch's book on his desk at the ministry in order to refer to it as frequently as possible.)

Educators like Sherrington and Stannard speak for many when they identify the problems as lying outside a simple knowledge v. skills paradigm. Joel Shatsky, a teacher in the US, speaks for many teachers when he says,

> I admire Hirsch's concern that there should be high standards in the curriculum as well as careful and abundant aids for new and struggling teachers. I only wish the typical school were able to provide the

resources and . . . guidance to follow such a program. But many schools can't and for a variety of reasons, much of which center around poverty: dilapidated school buildings, inadequate resources, lack of strong leadership by the principal, and poorly motivated children due to an environment unsupportive of learning.[24]

Since 2010, the coalition has encouraged radical changes to curricula and teaching practice within schools. In 2012 the government introduced a new accountability measure, the EBacc certificate. A new column was introduced in the school performance tables that ranked England's schools by how many students had achieved six GCSEs in English, maths, two sciences, a modern or ancient foreign language, history or geography. Not only did the new measure partially puncture the success of a number of previously successful schools but a DfE report revealed that the Ebacc measure 'led directly to a reduction in provision for creative subjects. 27 per cent of schools have withdrawn at least one subject as a result of the [measure]. Of these schools: Drama and Performing Arts have been withdrawn in 23 per cent of them; Art has been withdrawn in 17 per cent and Design Technology has been withdrawn in 14 per cent'.[25] The EBacc has now been replaced by the Best 8 accountability measure, still loosely based on the Ebacc subjects but designed to ensure a broader curriculum: too late, of course, for the already axed courses and the students who might have taken them.[26]

Reform to the curriculum has proven equally controversial. In 2013 two expert advisers to the government's curriculum review resigned in protest at the fact-heavy syllabi being proposed for very young children. There was a storm of criticism at what many believed to be a dangerous narrowing of the secondary school history curriculum. According to Cambridge's Professor Richard

Evans, 'Michael Gove's history curriculum is a pub quiz not an education'. Evans claimed that

> Michael Gove's new draft national curriculum for history . . . has been greeted with dismay by history teachers at every level . . . This is a curriculum that will produce a generation of young Britons with no knowledge of the history of any part of the world beyond the shores of the British Isles . . . the new curriculum tells pupils what to think.[27]

The decision to reduce the 'talk element' in the curriculum has been heavily criticised by Professor Robin Alexander, expert in primary education. Responding to a view expressed by minister Nick Gibb, at a seminar held within the Department in February 2012, that such an emphasis could encourage 'idle chatter in class' Alexander wrote,

> We say again here, as we said then, that those of us working in this field have long advanced something which is neither idle not mere chatter: an approach to spoken language that is rigorously planned and implemented; that engages and sustains children's attention to the task in hand; that challenges and stretches their thinking; that probes their understanding and misunderstanding, building on the one and rectifying the other; that demands as much of the teacher's expertise as it does of the child's developing linguistic skills.[28]

Peter Hyman has built his free school School21 around six principles, including 'eloquence', precisely because he believes that oracy is such an important skill. As Martin Robinson, writing in the TES, observes, 'Hyman is at the vanguard of an increasingly vocal group of teachers and educationalists who believe that oracy should be part of the curriculum – not just because it helps pupils to progress in life but for deeper, philosophical reasons'.[29] According to Hyman,

> for too many people it's about having a debate club after school. What we're about is putting oracy at the heart of our learning. In this school, lessons are filled with talk, discussion and debate. Our students are confident and articulate. We want oracy to be right up there with reading and writing.[30]

Ofsted judged School21 to be Outstanding in July 2014.[31] Inspectors praised the 'strong focus on oracy', the pupils' 'ability to talk fluently and accurately and express ideas' and the 'carefully planned, sharply focused termly projects set across subjects [which] provide high levels of challenge'. Talk and cross-curricular projects (usually derided by the anti-progressive lobby) were central to the success of School21.

More generally, there has been professional disquiet at the speed of many government educational reforms. Brian Lightman, leader of the Association of School and College Leaders (ASCL), argued that while heads shared the government's aspiration for high standards, the reforms were too much too fast. 'One year to implement such ambitious proposals effectively alongside the vast number of concurrent reforms is a tall order.'

Lightman also questioned the level of political involvement in the process.

> Drafting a curriculum is a highly specialised and professional task. Unlike previous versions of the national curriculum, which were drafted with a heavy involvement of teachers and school leaders, these proposals have been driven and closely directed by politicians without that professional input.[32]

According to Kevin Stannard, writers like Daisy Christodoulou indulge in caricature of contemporary 'subtle
thinkers . . . [such as] Ken Robinson, Chris Quigley, Guy
Claxton to name but three . . . [who are] drawn as extremists,
on the dark side of a Manichean world of good and
bad'.[33] Toby Young also launched a blistering attack on
Ken Robinson.[34]

Yet the more prosaic reality is that numerous 'progressive' projects within the state system are helping teachers
to raise standards, promote academic rigour and increase
pupil enjoyment. Some of the most detailed research into
effective teaching methods and 'styles' has been carried
out by the Sutton Trust and the Education Endowment
Foundation, who have evaluated 30 different school interventions in terms of how many months gain (or loss) it
produces for student. Many of the most effective fall under
approaches that would normally be seen as 'progressive'.
Feedback and meta-cognition strategies ('learning to learn')
top the list with a gain of 8 months. Peer tutoring results
in a six month gain and collaborative learning is plus five
months, as are oral language interventions and 'mastery
learning' which involve students learning at their own pace,
an approach started in the '60s. The only other approaches
giving five or more months benefit are early years intervention, one-to-one tuition and (at secondary level) homework.
In contrast some of the approaches of more traditional advocates are found to be among the least successful. Research
indicates neither performance-related pay nor school uni-
form have any benefit and setting actually has a negative
effect, especially on the mid-range and lower attaining
learners. Setting is, of course, very common in our schools
and it has been suggested that the next Conservative man-
ifesto would make it compulsory. Yet the research shows
that the only intervention that has a worse effect than setting is repeating a year. Based on the hard evidence, then,
from studies across the world, of what works in education

Progressive education lowers standards

it seems that it is the traditionalists, and not the progressives, who need to be questioning their approaches.[35]

And particular examples of progressive approaches yield similarly positive results. In the Learning Without Limits project, supported by Cambridge University, staff and researchers have tracked the innovative practice of Wroxham primary school in Hertfordshire. They wanted to know what happens when staff

> members jettison officially prescribed practices of predicting or pre-judging what any individual children might achieve? When they work, instead, to identify and lift limits on learning? When they replace the fatalism of ability labels with a more hopeful, powerful and empowering view of learners and learning?[36]

In this case, the answers were unequivocal: 'in just a few years, the school (once in special measures) grew into a thriving community, with distinctive views of learning, curriculum and pedagogy, monitoring and accountability, that found expression in every aspect of school life'.[37] In its June 2013 Ofsted inspection, Wroxham received an 'Outstanding' rating in every single category.[38]

At Stanley Park high school in Carshalton, Surrey, students have been taking part in collaborative based learning and project-based work, one of several pilot schemes organised by the Innovation Unit, originally a part of the Department for Education but now a separate social enterprise. Students are taught in unusual but interesting ways – with one Year 7 class working on a hardback (produced by the pupils' own publishing company) entitled *The horrible, miserable Middle Ages*. Listening to one student report his experiences, a *Guardian* reporter described 'facts . . . rushing out of Sam Goodwin almost as if he's unable to stop them'. School head David Taylor rejects the idea 'that because we're doing this, we don't value knowledge, that we have low expectations, that we're doing our children a disservice. Knowledge is important, don't get me wrong,' he says, 'But what's really important is how you apply it'.[39] Last year, the school's GCSE results improved dramatically.

In recent years, the Slow Education movement has been gaining ground in both the private and state school sector. As founder Maurice Holt writes,

> The notion of slow is essentially about establishing a process that fosters intensity and understanding and equips students to reason for themselves. An essential aim is fostering the ability to understand in depth, and the arts of deliberation are an essential element in this. In slow education, the concept of process is central to the way the curriculum is conceived and experienced: what is abhorrent is the notion of delivery, and this distinguishes the slow curriculum from one driven by outcomes.[40]

At Matthew Moss High School, Rochdale, the school has successfully implemented a 'slow education' model, stressing the importance of both students and teachers learning to take risks, make mistakes, learn from them – and move on. Rather than promoting a transmission model of education, slow education, in the words of the school's headmaster, teaches students that 'Learning is a bit unpredictable, is a personal experience and . . . the process of doing it is part of its value'. Above all, students are given time to complete their projects. As one student says, 'You learn more because you're interested in it' while a teacher makes it clear that it is not a short-term target-setting approach but ultimately 'it will [produce] people who operate much better in the world'.[41]

It is not just educators who are urging a less linear and backward-looking approach within our schools. A recent report from a group of businessmen and civic leaders, chaired by Sir Roy Anderson, a former rector of Imperial College, London, called for a new independent body of teachers, employers, academics and political parties to establish a long-term consensus on the school curriculum. According to the report, 'non-cognitive skills and attributes such as team working, emotional maturity and empathy . . . are as important as proficiency in English and mathematics'.[42]

There is then an urgent need to detoxify the current over-politicised atmosphere around teaching and learning. It has not only clouded the judgement of too many in power but prevented incremental improvement within state education. Even Robert Peal acknowledges the need for a middle way on this issue:

> Should children learn from the wisdom of an authoritative teacher, or should they learn independently and discover things for themselves? Should children learn an academic curriculum, or is this just filling their heads with 'mere knowledge' where 'skills' would be more useful? Should children be driven by the structure of rewards and examinations, or should they be motivated by lessons that are 'relevant' and 'fun'? Should children be sanctioned for misbehaving and not working, or is such a practice cruel and authoritarian? *For the moderate minded observer, it would seem that the obvious path lies through the middle of each of these statements.*[43]

Just so.

Notes

1 http://www.smf.co.uk/michael-gove-speaks-at-the-smf/ accessed 28 January 2015.
2 Robert Peal, *Progressively worse: The burden of bad ideas in British schools*, Civitas, 2014, p. xiv.

Progressive education lowers standards

3 Robert Peal, *Progressively worse: The burden of bad ideas in British schools*, Civitas, 2014, p. 210.

4 Robert Peal, *Progressively worse: The burden of bad ideas in British schools*, Civitas, 2014, p. 263.

5 Andrew Old, introduction to Robert Peal, *Progressively Worse: The burden of bad ideas in British Schools*.

6 Reproduced at http://www.historylearningsite.co.uk/great_debate. htm accessed 28 January 2015.

7 I am grateful to Patrick Yarker, co-editor of Forum for his clarity of analysis of the anti-progressive camp.

8 https://news.tes.co.uk/b/opinion/2014/05/29/review-39-the-entire-educational-landscape-is-obliterated-by-a-short-but-intensely-argued-book-39.aspx accessed 28 January 2015.

9 Robert Peal, *Progressively Worse: The burden of bad ideas in British schools*, Civitas, 2014, p. xiv.

10 http://civitas.org.uk/education/POTB.php accessed 28 January 2015.

11 http://blogs.spectator.co.uk/coffeehouse/2014/01/ofsted-vs-english-education/ accessed 28 January 2015.

12 https://debrakidd.wordpress.com/2013/07/06/7-myths-about-education-an-alternative-view/ accessed 17 August 2015.

13 http://www.smf.co.uk/media/news/michael-gove-speaks-smf/ accessed 28 January 2015.

14 http://www.primaryreview.org.uk/downloads/College_of_ Teachers_15.5.09.pdf accessed 28 January 2015.

15 http://www.smf.co.uk/media/news/michael-gove-speaks-smf/ accessed 28 January 2015.

16 http://www.robinalexander.org.uk/wp-content/uploads/2012/05/ Plowden-truth-and-myth.pdf accessed 28 January 2015.

17 Robert Peal, *Progressively worse: The burden of bad ideas in British schools*, Civitas, 2014, p. 94.

18 Brian Simon, *What future for education?* Lawrence and Wishart, 1992, p. 76.

19 Kevin Stannard http://news.tes.co.uk/b/opinion/2014/05/29/review-39-the-entire-educational-landscape-is-obliterated-by-a-short-but-intensely-argued-book-39.aspx accessed 28 January 2015.

20 http://headguruteacher.com/2013/08/05/a-perspective-on-seven-myths/ accessed 28 January 2015.

21 http://debrakidd.wordpress.com/2013/07/06/7-myths-about-education-an-alternative-view/ accessed 28 January 2015.

22 http://headguruteacher.com/2013/08/05/a-perspective-on-seven-myths/ accessed 17 August 2015.

23 http://www.coreknowledge.org/ed-hirsch-jr accessed 28 January 2015.

24 http://www.huffingtonpost.com/joel-shatzky/educating-for-democracy-e_b_411085.html accessed 28 January 2015.

139

Progressive education lowers standards

25 https://www.gov.uk/government/publications/the-effects-of-the-english-baccalaureate accessed 28 January 2015.

26 https://www.gov.uk/government/uploads/system/uploads/attachment_data/file/285990/P8_factsheet.pdf accessed 28 January 2015.

27 http://www.newstatesman.com/lifestyle/education/2013/03/rotesets accessed 28 January 2015.

28 http://www.robinalexander.org.uk/wp-content/uploads/2012/11/Alexander-Neither-national-nor-a-curriculum-Forum.pdf accessed 28 January 2015.

29 Martin Robinson, 'Utter brilliance', *Times Educational Supplement*, 4 July 2014, not available online.

30 Martin Robinson, 'Utter brilliance', *Times Educational Supplement* 4 July 2014, not available online.

31 http://www.ofsted.gov.uk/inspection-reports/find-inspection-report/provider/ELS/138196 accessed 28 January 2015.

32 http://www.bbc.co.uk/news/education-23222068 accessed 28 January 2015.

33 Kevin Stannard http://news.tes.co.uk/b/opinion/2014/05/29/review-39-the-entire-educational-landscape-is-obliterated-by-a-short-but-intensely-argued-book-39.aspx accessed 28 January 2015.

34 http://civitas.org.uk/education/POTB.php accessed 28 January 2015.

35 The Education Endowment Foundation Teaching and Learning Toolkit: http://bit.ly/1utojna accessed 28 January 2015.

36 http://learningwithoutlimits.educ.cam.ac.uk/creatinglwl/ accessed 28 January 2015.

37 http://learningwithoutlimits.educ.cam.ac.uk/creatinglwl/ accessed 28 January 2015.

38 http://www.thewroxham.org.uk/wp-content/uploads/2012/09/The-Wroxham-School-Ofsted-Report-June-2013.PDF accessed 28 January 2015.

39 http://www.theguardian.com/education/2014/feb/25/pisa-tables-assess-collaborative-problem-solving-michael-gove accessed 28 January 2015.

40 See more at: http://www.localschoolsnetwork.org.uk/2014/04/slow-education-possibilities-for-research-and-development/#sthash.8zYc11Io.dpuf accessed 28 January 2015.

41 http://sloweducation.co.uk/2013/06/10/a-slow-education-school-case-study-matthew-moss-high-school-rochdale/ accessed 28 January 2015.

42 http://www.theguardian.com/commentisfree/2014/feb/03/state-schools-independents-michael-gove accessed 28 January 2015.

43 Robert Peal, *Progressively worse: The burden of bad ideas in British schools*, Civitas, 2014, p. xiv.

Afterword

We founded the Local Schools Network for several reasons. We wanted to give a voice to parents who use and support their local schools. We wanted to celebrate the achievements of those schools and to remind people that local schools are more than just a vehicle for good solid educational achievement. They also knit communities together and enable children to understand diversity as well as to share their common humanity.

We also wanted to provide a place where we, and others, could dispel some of the myths and lies that are perpetuated on a daily basis about state schools by the media, and sadly by some politicians. These are myths and lies about how our schools are run, about what goes on in them and also about how they should be supported and improved where necessary.

We have recently had a general election in which, surprisingly, education figured very little in public debate, meaning many important questions about the shape of our schools, now and in the future, were simply not addressed.

Do we turn the clock back and recreate an era when academic selection blighted communities? Do we continue with the relentless fragmentation of local education, increasingly diminishing the role of local authorities and possibly introducing profit-making companies in the mix of providers? Are we going to see the teaching profession being downgraded into a job anyone can do, or can we make teaching the high status, high-skilled and respected profession it is in the world's most high-achieving nations? All these questions should be at the heart of local and national political discussion, particularly now as the Conservative government, elected in May 2015, presses forward with the dangerous fragmentation of our education system.

We hope that this book will help to bust the myths that have been deployed to create such damage, and foster well-informed debate on these critical issues. We hope it will give everyone with an interest in the future of our schools the evidence to make the case for *all* that we believe in at LSN.

And that is, above all, great teachers, excellent school leaders and flourishing local all-ability schools; answerable to their communities, challenged when necessary but always supported, recognised and celebrated as the rich community resource they can and should be.

Melissa Benn, Francis Gilbert,
Fiona Millar, Henry Stewart

Foreword to articles

The Local Schools Network was set up to promote the positive role of local schools by celebrating their achievements, building networks and to inform the public about key policy issues while providing a forum for debate. The four co-founders and Janet Downs (LSN's most prolific contributor) regularly write on a wide range of educational issues. Each of us comes to the education question from a unique and slightly different angle, whether it be as a teacher, ex-teacher, governor, parent activist or concerned grandparent. Between the five of us, we have written hundreds, if not thousands, of articles and posts on numerous aspects of contemporary educational policy over the last four years, both on the Local Schools Network and in a variety of national newspapers, magazines and journals.

We thought it would be interesting to include a brief sample of this more journalistic work, particularly those pieces that touch directly on the themes explored in this book. It was hard to choose only one article per person, but a key criteria was that the articles chosen should not overlap with or repeat material in the book, but instead elaborate and develop our arguments. We also wanted to convey a sense of the unique writing voice and different approach of each of us.

Want fairer school admissions? Then stop tinkering and scrap all selection

Fiona Millar

Over the past few weeks I have found myself unusually preoccupied with the issue of school admissions. Secondary open days are taking place all around me, and the subject is on many parents' lips.

Delving into the evidence about the so-called tutor-proof[1] 11-plus test (which is in fact nothing of the sort) and discovering that three-quarters of secondary schools[2] in England are now their own admissions authorities hasn't helped.

There is nothing new in this preoccupation – the first piece I wrote in *The Guardian* over 10 years ago was on the subject of inequities in the way school places are allocated. The rapid diversification of school types has only made the problem worse.

In that period I have also had the chance to lobby successive politicians and their advisers on admissions so I know that the two biggest culprits – selection by faith and ability – are off the table when it comes to further reform.

The response you get is broadly similar, regardless of their party. Pained expressions and sympathetic noises are swiftly followed by a short lecture on the realpolitik of trying to tackle these long-standing features of the English education system.

The third demon is residential geography and the power some parents have to worm their way, even fraudulently, into the most popular schools. This could be overcome by the routine use of random allocation (lotteries) but only if, and it is a big if, the notion of 'parent choice' wasn't so omnipotent.

And the problem is now becoming an open sore for the politicians. The focus on disadvantaged pupils, specifically those eligible for the pupil premium, sits increasingly uneasily with evidence about school intakes.

A recent internal analysis by the Department for Education of the top 100 non-selective schools apparently only reinforced what organisations such as the Sutton Trust and the British Humanist Association have been saying for years: the highest-performing schools take relatively few disadvantaged pupils compared to their local populations. But the latest solution, letting all schools rather than just academies and free schools prioritise those eligible for the pupil premium,[3] just seems another lame duck response to a chronic problem.

There is no evidence that schools really will seize this (voluntary) opportunity. No one seems to know how many academies and free schools have already chosen to, but I understand the DfE's research showed that none in the 'top 100' had.

There would be nothing to stop schools applying the pupil premium priority along with a number of other socially selective criteria, in effect cherry-picking the more able and aspirant disadvantaged children.

Ministers could make it a requirement for schools to prioritise pupil premium applicants in the same way that looked-after children are now automatically placed at the top of the list.

But then realpolitik interferes again. The pupil premium covers any child eligible for free school meals at any time in the preceding six years. The sheer volume of these pupils in some areas could rapidly distort entry to all local schools and cause parental uproar.

Moreover determining eligibility would be a nightmare. The DfE model free school admissions policy[4] suggests that parents should just vouch for their child's free meals status on a supplementary admissions application form. But who would take responsibility for gathering the evidence to back up these claims? What would happen to the children whose eligibility had virtually expired, or to those whose parents had simply lied?

Even if these obstacles could be overcome, a fast-track to the most sought-after school may not necessarily be the best choice. Some of these 'top' schools don't narrow achievement gaps significantly, while other lower flyers with more pupils eligible for free school meals have developed exemplary expertise in this area.

However this isn't just about achievement, it is also about the long-term implications for society of dividing children up in this way; of having schools where a concentration of better-off children are educated together, and the rest.

The Code of Practice[5] states clearly that school admissions shouldn't 'disadvantage unfairly, either directly or indirectly, a child from a particular social or racial group'. But that sort of discrimination is going on all the time.

Until the myriad forms of social and academic selection are eliminated altogether, and we adopt fairer systems such as random allocation and banding, which seeks to give every school across a given area broadly similar intakes, nothing much will change.

Pained expressions all round on reading this? Probably, but most people who study these matters know this is true and that simply slipping a few children eligible for the pupil premium through the net will make very little difference.

This article was first published by *The Guardian*/the guardian.com. Printed with kind permission of theguardian. com.

Notes

1   http://www.theguardian.com/education/2014/sep/16/state-school-pupils-worse-tutor-proof-11-plus-tests accessed 16 September 2015.
2   http://www.theguardian.com/education/2014/oct/07/choice-schools-children-parents-admissions-selection accessed 16 September 2015.
3   http://www.theguardian.com/education/2014/jul/22/state-schools-prioritise-disadvantaged-pupils-admissions-reform accessed 16 September 2015.
4   https://www.gov.uk/government/publications/free-schools-admissions accessed 16 September 2015.
5   https://www.gov.uk/government/publications/school-admissions-code accessed 16 September 2015.

An inside perspective

After a long career in the classroom, Francis Gilbert believes constant training is essential for anyone who wants to teach.

I've been teaching in various comprehensives for over twenty years now, but my training still shapes the way I teach. While some of the lectures on my Postgraduate Certificate in Education (PGCE) at Cambridge University in 1989 were a bit ropey, a great deal was invaluable. My training gave me a good grounding in how children learn; I was shown how to get children actively involved in learning by deploying strategies like group work, role play and directed activities related to texts. I did two student placements; one in Peterborough and one in Coventry. The inner-city school in Coventry was very challenging but I survived, and really benefitted from spending the last term reflecting upon what had happened to me in the university setting.

Considerably less teacher training goes on in universities now – PGCE programmes are being drastically cut – which

I think is a shame. I have noticed a qualitative difference between Graduate Teacher Programme (GTP) students who have been trained on the job, and those who've been based at a university for their training, who tend to have much better preparation in the relevant theories and teaching strategies. This, for me, is crucial. If you don't have an awareness of how children learn, of the ways in which various educational contexts shape and mould teacher and pupil identities, of what the different models of intelligence are, then you'll never gain an overview of what you're doing; you'll always be drowning in the minutiae that deluges schools on a daily basis.

I've seen quite a few poorly-trained teachers become obsessed with drilling students for exams because they don't know how children best learn; their lessons involved a lot of copying and sedentary learning. Sometimes these teachers can get very good exam results because their students follow their instructions carefully, but I worry that their pupils haven't really learnt much beyond absorbing the message that you get on by copying the teacher.

Now you may well be thinking, well, these teachers have got great results and didn't really need much training, so why bother with the whole thing?

Well, this is precisely where good training is crucial; if you have a good grounding in educational psychology, philosophy and history, you won't be flattered by your good exam results. You'll seek to get good results the 'right' way, by making your lessons interesting, engaging and relevant. You'll know how to assess your pupils' abilities on a holistic basis, you'll understand that intelligence is assessed by a lot more than exams and IQ tests.

Furthermore, you'll understand that the need for training is ongoing. A few years ago, I embarked upon a PhD in Creative Writing and Education at Goldsmiths College on a part-time basis while carrying on teaching at a secondary level.

Despite already being a successful teacher, the experience of working with academics who are experts in the educational field has improved my teaching further because it has made me reflect upon my practice as a teacher in a much more imaginative and analytical fashion.

I've revisited theorists from the past, and applied some of their lessons in the classroom. It's made me realise on quite a profound level that teachers are constantly learning, and training is vital if you're going to be an effective pedagogue.

This article was first published by www.totalpolitics.com. Printed with kind permission of www.totalpolitics.com.

Should schools compete or collaborate?

Henry Stewart

This could surely be a key dividing line between the main parties in the coming election. Should schools compete like businesses in the marketplace or should they collaborate for the common good?

Competition: no evidence of benefit

This week's Policy Exchange report[1] on free schools was clear on the underlying agenda. Evoking Milton Friedman, they explain that the idea behind free schools was that 'building new schools would create competition between schools by creating a surplus of places which would motivate schools to drive up standards and improve their provision'.

Opponents (ourselves included) have criticised the government for funding free schools where there is no need for more places. For Policy Exchange this is part of the point of free schools, to create surplus places and thus create competition. The IFS has supported this view, arguing in its paper 'Choice and Competition in Education Markets' that 'economic theory tells us that competition is what ensures consumers get a "good deal"'.

Policy Exchange are by no means neutral, being the original advocates of new independent state schools. However even they, after extensive study, could find no evidence[2] overall that competition from free schools brought any benefit to existing nearby schools. The IFS report[3] had already come to similar conclusions: 'a number of different studies have found no strong evidence to suggest that English schools with more competitors perform any better in terms of exam results'.

Fraser Nelson, writing last year in *The Spectator*, explained that the failures of free schools was nothing to be concerned about: 'There are 178 free schools; next year there'll be closer to 300. If you were to set up 300 new businesses, you'd expect at least 30 to hit trouble.' However there is a big difference between not being able to buy a coffee because your local cafe has shut down and the disruption to a child in finding their school has closed.

As my colleague Janet Downs has noted, before the last election Policy Exchange co-authored 'Blocking the Best', supporting for-profit schools. The first step was to create independent state schools, as free schools are. At its launch Michael Gove said[4] he would be happy to see groups like Serco running schools. And indeed Nick Clegg has claimed that it is only the fact that the Conservatives are in coalition that means we do not have for-profit schools in the English education system.

To support the case for competition, Policy Exchange quote research on the US, Sweden and Chile. One thing that these countries have in common are that none perform well in international comparisons (all being below England in the PISA tables). The Swedish experiment, a key inspiration for Gove's free schools, is now commonly described in terms such as 'Sweden's School Choice Disaster'.[5] An enquiry for the Swedish government[6] last year came to a clear conclusion that the experiment had failed.

The idea of school competition may work perfectly in (free market) theory. But the evidence seems clear: it doesn't seem to work in practice.

Collaboration between schools: a track record of success

The contrast with the benefits of collaboration is huge. The London Challenge was arguably this country's most successful educational project of the last 25 years, playing a key role in transforming the capital's schools. Led by Chief Adviser Tim Brighouse, it was always based on supporting schools and ensuring they worked together.

The Ofsted report[7] on London Challenge is clear on this. Key to the success were successful heads mentoring headteachers in target schools, support, 'without strings attached and without conflicts of interest' and teachers being committed to all London children not just those in their own school.

The Independent reported[8] this week on the transformation of schools in Basildon. From 7 primary schools rated 'Inadequate' two years ago, there are now none. The 14 rated 'Requires Improvement' are down to 9, with the expectation that, by next year, all Basildon schools will be rated Good or Outstanding.

The Basildon model, already being extended to other areas, is firmly based on all schools in the area – local authority and academy – working together, is based on co-operation, mentoring between schools, actively celebrating each other's successes and teachers being committed to all London children not just those in their own school.

Competition or collaboration?

Bringing competition and the private sector into public provision has been a major theme of the last few decades, whichever party has been in power. However I suspect I am not alone in finding it hard to think of a service that has been improved as a result of being run by G4S, Serco, Capita or others. Neither do I share the Tories' private sector good/public sector bad view in terms of customer service. As I prepare to make a call to Virgin Media that I know will involve waiting on hold for an hour, and probably lead to them failing to do what they promise, I only wish they had the efficiency and responsiveness that I experience when I call Hackney Council.

One journalist who interviewed me about the Policy Exchange report talked about trying to talk to a free school about their, in that case, good practice. They wouldn't let him visit and didn't want to have him describe what they do. Why? Because they saw it as a competitive advantage, and didn't want other schools to be aware of it.

That is a big contrast with what I experience as a Governor in Hackney. We do have a mix of academies and maintained schools but, like in Basildon, we work together in collaboration with the local authority. The local authority administers admissions to ensure they are fair. We regularly visit each other's schools to learn from best practice, mentoring takes place between the heads, and the schools work strategically on issues from exclusions to university admissions.

Schools collaborating: the opportunity for Labour

The Conservative position is clear. Their ideology leads them to believe that the driving force for school improvement has to be competition even though even their own supporters have to acknowledge – in England or in other countries – that there is little evidence that it works. I do not believe that the population shares their desire to have schools competing like business in a free market. For the

Greens, Caroline Lucas understands this very well – this week accurately describing the role of free schools as to 'marketise' education.

There is a big opportunity here for Labour. I believe parents prefer the idea of schools collaborating and sharing best practice, rather than competing – for mutual benefit. It makes sense and also fits with the evidence of what works. Let's hope Labour make this a very clear dividing line in the General Election.

This article was first published by The Local Schools Network. Printed with kind permission of www.local schoolsnetwork.org.uk.

Notes

1   http://www.policyexchange.org.uk/publications/category/item/a-rising-tide-the-competitive-benefits-of-free-schools accessed 16 September 2015.
2   http://www.localschoolsnetwork.org.uk/2015/03/free-schools-policy-exchange-finds-no-positive-effect-for-schools-nearby/ accessed 16 September 2015.
3   http://www.ifs.org.uk/economic_review/fp242.pdf accessed 16 September 2015.
4   http://www.localschoolsnetwork.org.uk/2011/10/gove-is-in-favour-of-profit-making-companies-running-state-schools/ accessed 16 September 2015.
5   http://www.slate.com/articles/news_and_politics/the_dismal_science/2014/07/sweden_school_choice_the_country_s_disastrous_experiment_with_milton_friedman.html accessed 16 September 2015.
6   http://www.swedishwire.com/politics/19371-why-swedens-educational-system-has-failed accessed 16 September 2015.
7   http://www.localschoolsnetwork.org.uk/2012/11/ofsted-contradicts-gove-success-of-london-challenge-had-little-to-do-with-sponsored-academies/ accessed 16 September 2015.
8   http://www.independent.co.uk/news/education/education-news/basildon-becomes-the-model-for-educational-excellence-as-scheme-turns-around-towns-schools-10102022.html accessed 16 September 2015.

Gove distorts history to 'prove' teenagers are ignorant of history

Janet Downs

'Survey after survey has revealed disturbing historical ignorance, with one teenager in five believing Winston Churchill
was a fictional character while 58 per cent think Sherlock
Holmes was real,' wrote Education Secretary Michael Gove.[1]

But when asked*, the Department for Education (DfE)
was unable to say what these surveys were. The DfE could
find only one: a survey done by UKTV Gold. But it didn't
have any further information.

So, not 'survey after survey' – just one. And that was
done by a TV company. The poll isn't on UKTV Gold's
website any more but after a bit of digging I found it here.[2]
The survey was 'specially commissioned' in 2008 by UKTV
Gold but it doesn't say who did it. The poll was designed to
test 'the nation on its historical knowledge by asking 3,000
people a series of questions relating to famous factual and
fictional characters'.

According to UKTV Gold, then, it tested 'the nation'.
That suggests a wider age range than just teenagers. But
what did these 3,000 people say? Results included:

> 21% thought that Churchill was fictional, 47% thought
> Richard the Lionheart didn't really exist and 23% believed
> Florence Nightingale was mythical.

58% thought Sherlock Holmes was real and 33% thought Biggles was an actual pilot.

It appears that the survey listed some characters and asked respondents to say which ones were real or fictional. The list was arbitrary and included some inaccuracies. For example, the survey listed Lady Godiva as fictional and said 12% believed she was real. But the 12% were right – Lady Godiva endowed monasteries at Stow and Coventry. And the 47% who thought 'fictional' Eleanor Rigby was real were no doubt thinking of Paul McCartney's anecdote that he found the name on a gravestone.

So, one rather dodgy survey of 3,000 people, not all teenagers, was used by Michael Gove to 'prove' that school leavers had inadequate historical knowledge.

Perhaps the survey should be updated and include a question about whether Orwell's Squealer[3] is fictional or not. Some people might answer that this master of propaganda is a real character who inhabits the DfE.

*Freedom of Information request can be viewed on WhatDoTheyKnow.com.

This article was first published by The Local Schools Network. Printed with kind permission of www.localschools network.org.uk.

Notes

1   http://www.dailymail.co.uk/debate/article-2298146/I-refuse-surrender-Marxist-teachers-hell-bent-destroying-schools-Education-Secretary-berates-new-enemies-promise-opposing-plans.html accessed 16 September 2015.
2   http://web.archive.org/web/20080509062051/http:/uktv.co.uk/gold/stepbystep/aid/598605 accessed 16 September 2015.
3   http://www.teachersmonthly.com/wp-content/uploads/2010/06/ENG-Animal-Farm-Propaganda-worksheet.pdf accessed 16 September 2015.

We need to tackle brazen elitism to help poorer children

Melissa Benn[1]

Michael Gove peddled the myth that poverty does not damage children's chances, says Melissa Benn.

Michael Gove has bequeathed the nation several tricky, and highly emotive, legacies. But perhaps none is more potent – apparently plausible and yet subtly dangerous – than the simplistic idea that education can be a universal route out of poverty.

The argument goes something like this: if schools can only get it right, then every child can escape his or her background or, at the very least, jump up a social class or two.

No one doubts that education can profoundly affect an individual life course. The poor pupil made good, thanks to the 11-plus, remains one of the most romantic cultural narratives of post-war Britain. During New Labour's time in office, 'aspiration' became the favoured, if rather more amorphous, buzzword. The 2009 Milburn report on fair access to the professions, for example, made much of the right of parents to get their children into a better school, while failing to make clear what should happen to those unlucky enough to remain stuck in a worse one.

Gove brought both rhetorical passion and political bad temper to this ongoing debate and a similarly impatient yet evangelical tone can be detected in the mission statements of Gove-era organisations, from Teach First to the free school movement to the tougher-minded academy chains.

The power of this collective message has long relied on a cynical caricature of comprehensive mediocrity. Poor children, we are told, have been held back by an army of inadequate teachers in the grip of progressive methods and the 'soft bigotry of low expectations'. Sweep away 'the blob', get every child a clutch of good GCSEs and a place at university and the class cards will be decisively shuffled.

Not so, according to a thoughtful new study[2] on education and social mobility by academics Kate Hoskins[3] and Bernard Barker.[4] Based on in-depth interviews with 88 children in two high-performing academies – schools with socially mixed intakes, strong teaching and excellent results – it asks some acute questions of this unrealistic narrative that has held sway for so long.

What Hoskins and Barker uncover is a complex, and poignant, picture of today's schools and the educational mindset that reigns there. Almost all the pupils interviewed believe that future exam and work success will depend almost entirely on their own hard work. Yet it is resoundingly clear just how much their choices, chances and prospects are shaped, and so often constrained, by family background on the one hand and wider economic forces on the other.

Far from breaking down social divisions, the vast majority of schools confirm them. From the moment they arrive at secondary school, children are academically sorted, usually along clear class lines. Even at high-performing schools, poorer children are still less likely to get GCSE results that are as good as their more affluent classmates'.

Parents' education and work inevitably has a strong influence on children's choices, but often in a surprisingly positive sense, with young people keen to do similar things to their mums and dads – as long as they are paid well and can live happy lives – rather than to escape into more glamorous, wealthier circumstances.

Meanwhile, professional families pass down all sorts of advantages to their offspring. This even includes the right to fail, as an interesting new study from the National University of Distance Learning confirms; middle-class children get second and third chances that are denied their poorer classmates. None of this is an argument for static or low expectations. But it does force us to recognise that schools can only do so much and that, unless other changes are put in place, the elite will always find a way to reproduce itself.

As Barker puts it pithily, 'If every child got into a Russell Group university, then there wouldn't be such a thing as a Russell Group university . . .' Some new hierarchy would emerge. Already, many poorer pupils are being channelled into lower-status universities yet often end up paying the same crippling fees as their better-off peers.

The OECD (Organisation for Economic Co-operation and Development) states unequivocally that if education is to make a real difference, fairer school systems have to go hand in hand with policies to enhance economic equality. Since 2010, coalition policy has widened the gap between rich and poor.

Even so, I cannot recall a single example of Gove or his allies publicly conceding that poverty has a significant impact on educational outcomes, or admitting the brazen elitism of our school system. Historians will judge these silences to be as politically significant as any dazzling set piece speech or ritual bit of 'blob' bashing.

Notes

1 http://www.teachersmonthly.com/wp-content/uploads/2010/06/ ENG-Animal-Farm-Propaganda-worksheet.pdf accessed 16 September 2015.
2 http://www.bookdepository.com/Education-Social-Mobility-Kate-Hoskins/9781858566139 accessed 16 September 2015.
3 http://www.roehampton.ac.uk/staff/Kate-Hoskins/ accessed 16 September 2015.
4 https://www.ioe.ac.uk/services/64972.html accessed 16 September 2015.

Index

Index

Core Curriculum 25–6, 28; Hirsch's view 131; Plowden Report 129; reform 132–3, 134; Slow Education movement 137
The Curriculum Centre (TCC) 25–6, 28

D'Ancona, Michael 23
Department for Education (DfE) 26; academies 24, 27, 35–6, 76, 85, 87–8, 90–1, 92; auditing accounts 34; free schools 29, 64; history surveys 156–7; matched funding 25; Pupil Premium 145, 146; school places 31
deprived areas 9, 10, 38, 63, 66, 77
Dewey, John 127, 128
didactic methods 128, 129
Director of School Standards (DSS) 37
disadvantaged pupils 15, 145; see also deprived areas
discipline 30–1, 125, 126
Discovery New School 60, 98
discrimination 146
'diverse providers' 22
Dobbie, W. 48
Downs, Janet 143, 152, 156–7
downward mobility 15
Dulwich School 116
Durand Academy Trust 69
Durham Free School 61

E-Act 61, 84–5
Economic Intelligence Unit (EIU) 52
Education Act (1902) 22
Education Act (1944) 4, 23
Education Act (2002) 11
Education Endowment Foundation (EEF) 51, 135
Education Funding Agency (EFA) 33–4, 59

The Education Network (TEN) 78
Education Reform Act (1988) 24
11+ examination 4–5, 6, 8, 9, 144
Elliott, Adrian 5
employment 14
English Baccalaureate (EBacc) 85–6, 132
equality of opportunity 16, 115, 120
equivalent exams 83–5, 86, 88–9
ethnic minorities 8–9, 48, 52, 66
Evans, Natalie 62–3
Evans, Richard 132–3
evidence-based pedagogy 103
examinations 69, 130, 149; 11+ examination 4–5, 6, 8, 9, 144; equivalent 83–5, 86, 88–9; see also GCSE results
extra curricula activities 110

faith schools 67, 68
feedback 135
Finland 3, 95, 98–9
free school meals 63, 145–6
free schools 11, 29, 43–4, 56–75, 154, 159; accounts 33; competition 151; conversion of private schools 117; failure of 152; funding 63–5, 66, 151; profit 45; Pupil Premium 145, 146; scandals 60–1; school places 31; services 31–2; Sweden 45–7, 52; unqualified teachers 96, 97, 98, 106–7
Freedman, Sam 11–12, 114–15
freedom 29–31
Freire, Paulo 127, 128
Friedman, Milton 151
Fryer, R. 48
funding: academies 77, 80; free schools 63–5, 66, 151; matched 25; Pupil Premium 63, 145–6; teacher training 100

Index

international studies 3, 52; *see also* PISA
Isle of Sheppey Academy 84, 116

Japan 3
Jenkins, Simon 5-6

Keates, Chris 66
Kidd, Debra 127-8, 130
Kings Science Academy 60-1
knowledge 101-2, 126, 129, 130, 131, 137
Knowledge Is Power Program (KIPP) 48
Kunskapsskolan 28
Kynaston, David 111, 113, 120
Kynaston, George 111

Labour: academies 44, 76, 77, 81, 87, 91; 'aspiration' as buzzword 158; comprehensive education 6, 10; curriculum 27; opportunity for 155; private schools 115, 116; *Putting Students and Parents First* 35-6; selective education 1-2; social mobility 12-13; teachers 105
league tables 27, 69-70, 110, 117-18
The Learning Curve (2012) 52-3
Learning Schools Trust (LST) 28
Learning Trust 38
Learning Without Limits 136
Lehain, Mark 61
Lightman, Brian 134
Little, Tony 70
'Local, Equal, Excellent' 8-9
local authorities 22-42, 141; accountability 33; admissions 32, 154; 'all-in' schools 6; auditing accounts 33-4; budgets 24-6; closing schools 29; curriculum 26-8; free schools 29; protection 32;

pupil and parent champions 35; school freedom 29-31; school places 31; services 24-5, 31-2; special educational needs 34; support from 9-10, 32-3; welfare 34-5
Local Government Association (LGA) 35
Local Management of Schools (LMS) 24
Local Schools Network 37, 60, 82-3, 103, 141, 143, 155, 157
London: academies 90; free schools 62, 63, 64, 65; local authorities 38; London Challenge 10, 32, 91-2, 153
London Oratory 68
London School of Economics (LSE) 13, 81, 87
'looked-after' children 68
Lucas, Caroline 154-5
Luckhurst, Tim 13

Machin, Stephen 81-2, 87
marketing 68-9
marketisation 18, 51, 67, 155
Marlborough College 111
mastery learning 135
matched funding 25
mathematics 27, 46, 48
Matthew Moss High School 137
McInerney, Laura 49-50, 57-8, 71
McKinsey 95
media headlines 1
mentoring 153, 154
meta-cognition 135
middle-class students 5, 11, 111, 160
Milburn report (2009) 158
Millar, Fiona 37, 117-18, 144-7
Mortimore, Peter 36, 101-2, 106
Mulberry school 115

Nash, John 25-6, 59, 62, 98
National Audit Office (NAO) 29, 31-4, 62, 64, 69, 80-1

Index

Index

testing 43, 69–70
Thatcher, Margaret 6, 127
Todd, Selina 10, 15, 17
Tomlinson, George 36
Tower Hamlets 38, 63, 115
traditionalism 124, 127, 128, 131, 135–6
Trojan Horse affair 69
Truss, Elizabeth 25, 27, 30
Turner, Jenny 56
tutoring 8
Tyndale, William 127

UKIP 18
UKTV Gold survey 156–7
United Learning 116
United States 2, 44, 47–50, 52, 152
universities 7, 10, 100, 109, 148–9
unqualified teachers 95–8, 102, 104–5, 106–7, 110

value added 90, 91
Vine, Sarah 17

vocational education 12, 83–4, 125

The Warren school 88
welfare 34–5
Wellington College 97, 111, 116
West Grantham Academies Trust (WGAT) 29
West London Free School 65
West London Free School Primary 63
Westminster Academy 115
Wilby, Peter 111
Wilshaw, Michael 11
Woessmann, Ludger 52
Wood, Alan 38
working-class students 5, 7, 10
Wroxham primary school 136

Young, Toby 24, 65, 119, 126, 127, 135

169